The Practical Executive and Leadership

D A Y L E M . S M I T H , P H . D .

Professor of Management
McLaren School of Business
University of San Francisco

Series Editor, Arthur H. Bell, Ph.D.

Printed on recyclable paper

NTC Business Books
a division of *NTC Publishing Group* • Lincolnwood, Illinois USA

HD
57.7
S647
1997

Library of Congress Cataloging-in-Publication Data

Smith, Dayle M.
    The practical executive and leadership / Dayle M. Smith.
       p.   cm.
    Included bibliographical references and index.
    ISBN 0-8442-2980-6 (alk. paper)
    1. Leadership.   I. Title.
HD57.7.S64 1997
658.4'092–DC20   96-38713
                                                              CIP

Published by NTC Business Books, a division of NTC Publishing Group
4255 West Touhy Avenue
Lincolnwood (Chicago), Illinois 60646-1975, U.S.A.
© 1997 by NTC Publishing Group. All rights reserved.
No part of this book may be reproduced, stored in a retrieval system,
or transmitted in any form or by any means,
electronic, mechanical, photocopying, recording or otherwise,
without the prior permission of NTC Publishing Group.
Manufactured in the United States of America.

6 7 8 9 0 VP 9 8 7 6 5 4 3 2 1

Contents

Foreword

> *The wicked leader is one whom the people despise. The good*
> *leader is one whom the people revere. The great leader is*
> *one of whom the people say, "We did it ourselves."*

Lao Tsu

Sex aside, no subject has fascinated the human race so often and for so long as inquiries into the nature of leaders and leadership. Egyptian hieroglyphics for leader (*seshemu*) and leadership (*seshemet*) appeared more than 5,000 years ago. Greek epics, including the *Iliad* and the *Odyssey*, are virtual case studies of the perils and potentials of leadership. During the Renaissance, Machiavelli warned in *The Prince* (1513) that "there is nothing more difficult to take in hand, more perilous to conduct, or more uncertain in its success, than to take the lead in the introduction of a new order of things."

In our era, hundreds of books and thousands of articles have been devoted to the search for understanding how leaders rise to authority, how they influence others while in power, and what forces lead to their fall. In her portion of this broad canvas, Dayle Smith has drawn together an especially helpful description of *what leaders do* in modern organizations. Her lucid analysis of five core leadership roles applies to leaders at all levels, from the boardroom to the ball field.

Leadership theorists have sought for years to specify an inclusive list of the central roles of leadership. (Some of these lists, or taxonomies/itemize more than one hundred supposedly distinct roles for leaders.) Smith cuts through such unwieldy complications in her insightful five-category treatment of what leaders do.

Leaders and would-be leaders can grasp these five roles quickly to increase their chances for success in business and other organizations.

Smith teaches how the roles of Vision, Relationship, Control, Encouragement, and Information apply to leaders at all levels. Her "Leadership Tips" in each chapter capture the essence of her points and give leaders a specific "to-do" list of best leadership practices.

Smith's approach to leadership roles can be tested by the exclusion principle: which of the many leadership activities she describes can be safely excluded from a leader's daily repertoire of skills? I believe the answer is *none*.

Here a leader or leader-in-training can find a complete, yet succinct guide to the crucial skills that matter most for leadership success at all levels in companies and organizations of all types and sizes.

Arthur H. Bell Ph.D.
McLaren School of Business
University of San Francisco
January 1996

Preface

This is a book written *for* busy leaders, not *about* them. Throughout, I have tried to direct ideas and guidelines to the broad range of leaders and leaders-to-be in companies, government organizations, professional societies, political parties, civic clubs, religious organizations, and hometown committees.

The book contains new ways of organizing what leaders do. Each of these roles is explained in detail, with supporting data, opinions, and war stories from a wide range of corporate and organizational leaders.

Just as valuable for leaders, I believe, are the scores of practical guidelines distributed throughout the book in the "Leadership Tips" features. These do's and don'ts, based on a wealth of recent leadership research, can set any leader onto a promising path for achieving organizational goals while avoiding unnecessary pitfalls.

My research for this work has taken me to more than fifty companies, dozens of organizations, and many smaller groups. I especially want to single out leaders at all levels in the following companies and organizations for generously sharing their insights with me about the challenges and fruits of leadership: American Stores, Artex Knitting Mills, Central Intelligence Agency, Companion Health Insurance, Cost Plus World Market, Inc., Fried & Sher, U.S. Coast Guard, New York University Executive Programs, Kaiser Permanente, Lucky Stores, U.S. State Department, Colonial Williamsburg Foundation, Johnson & Johnson Medical Instruments, PaineWebber, General Electric, Sun Microsystems, Charles Schwab, Wells Fargo, Los Angeles Times, Electroventure, Inc., Marriott Corporation, DuPont, Critikon, Pacific Bell, Deutsche Telekom, and IBM.

Finally, I wish to thank the following individuals at the McLaren School of Business for their support and encouragement with this work: Gary Williams, Dean; Denis Neilson, Associate Dean; and Eugene Muscat, Associate Dean. I would also like to thank my faculty colleagues at the University of San Francisco, Georgetown University, and the University of Southern California.

Dedicated to two future leaders, my daughters Lauren Elizabeth and Madeleine Alexis.

Dayle M. Smith
Belvedere, California
January, 1996

Leadership and the Right Stuff

One of the most universal cravings of our time is a hunger for compelling and creative leadership. . . . Leadership is one of the most observed and least understood phenomena on earth.

James MacGregor Burns,
Leadership[1]

Bob W., 26 years old, faces a career dilemma. After completing a master's degree in electrical engineering in 1993, he joined the new product development team at Global Computer. He worked hard and contributed to the team's success and prestige within the company. Yesterday his boss called him aside and offered him a promotion—a position as manager of a new product line.

Bob isn't sure what to say. On the one hand, he's complimented by the offer and attracted by the challenges of the new position. On the other hand, Bob wonders if he's cut out for this kind of leadership position. He wasn't class president in high school or an officer in his college fraternity. He doesn't consider himself a dynamic personality and, in fact, often experiences "speaker's nerves" during his occasional presentations in meetings and conferences. "Do I have the right stuff?" he ponders. "Isn't it true that leaders are born, not made?"

Bob's questions are common to us all as we face "crossroads moments" in life—the crossroads of deciding to lead or to follow. These moments occur in our careers, of course, but also in our civic, social, and personal lives.

This book is written for people at the
of leadership. Like Bob, some individuals
contemplating a promotion into a leadership po
Others may already find themselves facing leadership
responsibilities and wondering if they're right for the
challenges of the job. Still others are turning these
pages to learn as much as possible about the best
practices in leadership.

For all such readers, the central message of the
book can be stated simply: **leadership skills can be
described and learned. The key to leadership lies
not in *having* the right stuff from birth, but in
getting it.**

Put another way, leaders are seldom "born" to lead
in all circumstances of their personal and professional
lives. (If this were the case, leaders would be deter-
mined solely by parentage, and books on leadership
would focus primarily on genetics.) No matter what our
lineage, we each have opportunities from time to time
to step forward from the crowd and emerge as leaders.
We can seize those opportunities if we know what
leaders *do*.

So what is the "right stuff," mythic or otherwise?
As the Suggested Readings section of this book attests,
near-libraries have been devoted to this subject. In a
sentence:

> Leaders have the ability to develop a vision,
> the skill to articulate that vision in practical
> terms, and the skill to direct and assist others
> in executing the various aspects of that vision.

If leaders aren't born with these capacities, where
do they get them? How do you *do* leadership? A few
examples from history are instructive:

- Abraham Lincoln failed numerous times, in
  both business and politics, before becoming one of the great leaders of American
  history.

- F. W. Woolworth, the retailing giant of the
  late nineteenth and early twentieth centu-
  ries, went bankrupt several times before
  establishing one of the largest retail chains
  in the United States.

- Before Winston Churchill became the great
  British prime minister who led his country
  out of the darkest days of World War II,
  he directed one of the greatest military
  disasters of World War I, the Battle of
  Gallipoli. Also, from 1924 to 1929, as
  Chancellor of the Exchequer, he was
  responsible for a financial policy that
  created near-total disaster for the British
  stock market.

- Lee Iacocca brought Chrysler from bank-
  ruptcy to the best financial footing it had
  been on for half a century. Prior to that
  his career at Ford was marked by both
  success and failures, the last one being his
  dismissal.

What do all of these leaders have in common?
They learned from experience to *become* leaders.

Addressing Leaders at All Levels

This book does not attempt to rehearse, in textbook fashion, the close details of leadership research. Instead, the fruits of such research—the practical "so what?" for leaders and leaders in training—are gathered here and displayed in meaningful order, together with insights from my own investigations and the reflections of successful leaders. This book can serve the busy reader as a how-to summary of best practices in contemporary leadership, made memorable through scores of real-life leadership cases and anecdotes featuring political, business, civic, and social leaders.

Although the national and international "stars" of leadership are cited often here, the principles and techniques treated in this book also apply to leaders at all levels, from office supervisors to P.T.A. and civic leaders. The book is also intended for use by *followers* in organizations of all kinds—followers who have every reason to understand the efforts of their leaders. Knowing what a leader is up to, after all, can motivate followers to support his or her initiatives.

The best way to use the dozens of ideas and guidelines contained in this book is to *try them out* in a variety of business and social environments. The concepts in this book will become powerful components of your day-to-day life as you act upon them in real-world circumstances.

This book is organized to encourage that kind of use. Each chapter opens with an insight into a special aspect of leadership from a noted leader. That is followed by a brief scenario depicting an everyday situation faced by a leader or leader-in-the-making. The body of each chapter includes additional insights, guidelines, anecdotes and suggestions garnered from the best thinking, research, and time-tested practices from all over the world.

To make these guidelines and suggestions as accessible as possible, a section of "Leadership Tips" has been included at the end of each chapter.

A concluding note: if you feel your own visionary powers are at low ebb, read and think about the many leadership success stories that fill the following chapters. Success breeds success primarily because it restores vision and imagination.

Leadership Tips

1. Practice leadership skills at all levels of life responsibilities. What works at home also works at the highest corporate levels.

2. Experiment with leadership skills that do not come naturally for you. These techniques become valuable to you and your career only when you use them, not merely know about them.

3. Learn about leadership to understand *following* more deeply. Knowing who's driving the bus and why he or she is driving it can help you ride with more comfort—or decide which bus to take!

2

Three Myths
of Leadership

*I have read of men born peculiarly endowed
by nature to be a general . . . but I have never
seen one.*

General William Tecumseh Sherman

Hermann Hesse, in *Journey to the East,* tells the story of a group of men making an arduous cross-continent journey, under the sponsorship of a Holy Order. Even in their most difficult moments they are sustained and cheered by their servant, Leo, who faithfully performs their menial chores and keeps their spirits up by his songs and stories. The journey goes reasonably well until, inexplicably, Leo disappears. The group quickly falls into bickering factions. Before long, the journey is abandoned.

One member of the group, after years of wandering alone, stumbles upon Leo, who takes him into the protection of the Order that had sponsored the original journey. The wanderer is dumbfounded to discover that Leo, far from being a menial servant, has all along been the revered leader of the Order.

The true leaders—those who hold enterprises together and keep spirits high—wear no standard uniform of personality and spring from no single heritage. For every traditional leader at the head of the parade, there is another leader like Leo in Hesse's story, avoiding the limelight and choosing to lead by serving.

Understanding that leaders come in all flavors and sizes frees us to contemplate our own eligibility for leadership roles. Those who dislike the spotlight can learn to lead in less high-profile, but no less valuable ways. Those who, in President Harry Truman's words, "can't stand the heat" don't have to stay out of the kitchen. They can remodel the kitchen (or, in the current lingo, *reengineer* it) for their own comfort and efficiency as leaders.

CHANGING OUR MINDS ABOUT LEADERSHIP

The process of understanding leadership in all its human diversity begins by discarding three tired myths about leaders. These myths are hazardous because they *tempt us to exclude ourselves* from the candidate list for leaders.

Worse, these leadership myths distort the nature of true leadership and encourage "slaves" to accept a false idea that creates undesirable "masters" and, in the process, inhibits the development of would-be leaders.

THE BIRTHRIGHT MYTH: "LEADERS ARE BORN, NOT MADE."

This myth has deep and tangled cultural roots. The widespread belief that leaders either "have it" or don't from their earliest years springs in part from more than two thousand years of literature emphasizing the role of the *hero* (or, in an interesting hyperbole, the *super* heroes of contemporary films and video games).

In the great majority of these works of imagination or retold history, the hero is distinguished from fellow men and women by innate superior strength, courage, wisdom, physical attractiveness, and virtue. The list is long and familiar: Beowulf, King Arthur, El Cid, Tamerlaine, Alexander the Great, Richard the Lion-Hearted, and Joan of Arc, down to our own heroic historical figures such as Washington, Lincoln, Daniel Boone, Davy Crockett, Susan B. Anthony—not to mention Batman, Bruce Lee, and Steven Segal.

It is characteristic of all such heroes in this tradition that neither they nor their followers can explain the roots of the hero's superiority (except, perhaps, through divine parentage or "royal blood" in older legends), nor can such superbeings transfer their heroic abilities to others. They present themselves as unique individuals, and essentially mysterious beings—"above the common herd," in Byron's phrase.

This myth is dangerous when applied to leaders in businesses and other organizations. When we deify our leaders as men and women essentially unlike and superior to the rest of us, we undercut any organizational efforts at leadership development and transition planning. Where do you sign up for training to become a company god?

Granted, we usually do not *consciously* think of our company or organizational leaders as unalloyed heroes. But we often perpetuate the birthright tradition whenever we look upon our leaders as "naturals" for their positions—endowed, in short, by some genetic or early childhood history to be a hammer, rather than a nail, in business and society.

As we shall see in the following pages, many of the most prominent leaders reveal that far from being "naturals" for leadership positions, they had to *learn* to lead, often by painful lessons of trial and error. In their well-known interviews of 60 top-level corporate leaders and 30 leaders of public sector organizations for their book *Leaders: The Strategies for Taking Charge* (1985), Warren Bennis and Burt Nanus did not find themselves meeting a uniform series of Charlton Heston personalities. Instead, "there was a great amount of diversity among the leaders. . . . Most were very ordinary in appearance, personality, and general behavior."[2]

One of the most prominent leadership theorists of our century, Ralph Stodgill, undertook a painstaking review of scholarly works on leadership only to conclude that "a person does not become a leader by virtue of the possession of some combination of traits."[3]

Contrary to the Birthright Myth, leaders turn out to be people remarkably like the rest of us, but with the difference that *they know the skills and techniques of leadership*. This fact should be heartening for those taking the first steps toward leadership responsibilities in their organizations. If you don't feel you were born with the full set of leadership tools, don't despair. Neither was anyone else.

THE FOR-ALL-SEASONS MYTH:
"ONCE A LEADER, ALWAYS A LEADER."

Allied to the Birthright Myth is the inaccurate but widely held belief that certain people are everywhere, at all times, capable of assuming the challenges of leadership, no matter what the circumstances. The Birthright Myth attributes such talent to heritage; the For-All-Seasons Myth attributes it to character and track record.

Perhaps you have observed this myth in action at a P.T.A. election meeting or similar civic event. When the need for a vice president or other office is announced, all eyes turn to Mr. or Ms. Prominent Leader, no matter what his or her time availability or suitability for the position. We make the unwarranted assumption that a leader who is successful in one sphere—business, let's say—will be equally successful in social or civic leadership.

Just the opposite is often the case. When leaders are drawn away from their areas of strength and become overcommitted with unfamiliar responsibilities, they serve neither their followers nor themselves well. The problem of leaders saying yes to too many nominations and requests is not the fault of leaders alone; followers, after all, have *asked* the same people over and over to perform leadership tasks that often are beyond their abilities, interests, and time limitations.

We can gain a fairer view of leadership using the "crinkle" metaphor. Imagine a flat sheet of aluminum foil lying on a table before you. The question is this: as you begin to use your hands to crinkle the foil, where will the ridges and high points of foil emerge? The answer, of course, depends on *circumstances,* including where you chose to grasp the foil and how you crinkled it. After crinkling, the pattern of peaks and valleys of foil are unique to the circumstances that generated them. Even if you tried, you probably could not repeat the same pattern of folds, buckles, and creases in the foil.

In a similar fashion, leaders can emerge from the unique circumstances of the moment. No myth about a person's past or present status as a leader should keep us from considering others, or ourselves, as potential leaders.

This point is made eloquently in the true story of a jetliner crash in the Andes in 1972 (the basis of Piers Paul Read's novel, *Alive,* and a movie by the same title). The 28 survivors of the crash found themselves hopelessly marooned in an isolated, snowbound mountain valley, with only a broken section of the airplane fuselage for protection.

Several of the crash survivors with considerable leadership experience were, ironically, the first to perish as cold, hunger, and fear gripped the group. A previously shy, self-conscious boy named Parrado—an unlikely leader indeed, by traditional predictors— emerged as one of the most trusted and loved leaders among the trapped passengers, and the leader perhaps most responsible for their eventual survival.

Management guru John W. Work, senior principal in Work Associates, Inc., points out that leaders like Parrado often emerge in response to the needs of the moment and circumstance.

> Two general types of causes give rise to leadership. The first type may be called the *perceived-inequity* cause. This cause typically grows out of perceived inequities across diverse groups in corporate and organizational workplaces, communities, and other societal arenas. The second type of cause may be called the *search-for-excellence* cause. Here, corporate managers, organizational heads, and community and government officials with positions of responsibility and authority may perceive a need and be motivated to raise and improve an organization's level of efficiency, production and delivery of goods and/or services, and profitability.[4]

But *which* leaders will emerge to address inequities or pursue the search for excellence in your organization? That question must remain open to include the full range of stakeholders in any given situation. No one, in short, should be anointed from the beginning as the "DL"—designated leader—for any and all organizational needs. Circumstances may dictate that someone from the crowd—you or I, for example—may be the best leaders for the situation at hand.

When we believe in the possibility that anyone can be a leader, we create the social and intellectual climate in which the best leaders for the moment can step forward.

THE INTENSITY MYTH: "LEADERS ARE MORE EMOTIONALLY INTENSE THAN THE REST OF US."

This myth is based on the notion that great leaders feel things more broadly or deeply—are more emotionally intense—than the rest of us mere mortals.

Just as the range of human emotions is extensive, so too this myth takes many forms. Probably the best-known or most common is the Anger Myth—the idea that the boss is mad and we had better watch our step. In some companies, of course, the Anger Myth *is* a living, breathing reality in the form of a loud, dyspeptic manager. But is anger or other intense emotion the generally shared characteristic of all or most leaders?

No. The Anger Myth stems from the old belief that workers hate what they do and must be driven by the stick of anger to put in an honest day's work. This assumption about work and workers has been labeled "Theory X" by Douglas McGregor in *The Human Side of Enterprise*. Theory X managers, as typified by sweatshop bosses and the many industrialists depicted in Charles Dickens's novels are usually described as hard-driving, even cruel individuals whose general mood ranges from sour to apoplectic.

In this view, workers are supposedly motivated to do what they hate (their jobs) by the ever-present threat of explosive anger and related punishments from their employer. Fear is the electricity that powers Theory X organizations, and the dynamo generating that fear is the Captain Bly or Scrooge in the chief executive's chair.

Some U.S. business magazines, notably *Fortune,* have perpetuated the Anger Myth in annual features such as "The Ten Toughest Bosses in America." The adjectives used to describe these bosses are revealing: *no-nonsense, hard-driving, impatient, quick-tempered, mercurial, curt, brusque,* and *moody.* It would be easy to conclude from such articles that business leaders simply have to get mad and stay mad to motivate their work forces.

Although jolts of fear can electrify performance in any organization over the short term, it turns out that in most cases the angry leader self-destructs (often to the relief of bruised workers)—and often leaves considerable wreckage, if not total destruction, at his or her passing. In addition, the brightest and best in the work force want to be treated well. They don't work for long for a boss whose emotional repertoire is limited to anger, sullenness, and sarcasm. In fact, the personal cost of anger in executive ranks was made clear by the Dartmouth Heart Study in 1990, which identified anger as the single largest contributor to a variety of heart ailments.[5]

The Intensity Myth extends to emotional intensity in many forms. One notion of leadership holds that the true leader exudes more *confidence* than ordinary mortals; another suggests that the leader is more consistently *optimistic* than others or is more *passionate* about opinions and beliefs.

All such "extraordinary-emotional-state" tions of leadership have been contradicted than five decades of research. No significant study has identified a single emotional attribute as the common element among successful leaders. As a result, the many attempts to define what leaders *are* (as described by their emotional tendencies) have been superseded by more objective and successful studies of what leaders *do.*

Leaders and leaders in training should not attempt to display one emotional facade (whether of anger, confidence, or optimism), as if that front alone would a leader make.

Leadership Tips

1. Don't fall for the Birthright Myth. Leaders are *made,* and usually *self-made.*

2. See through the For-All-Seasons Myth. No one is or can be a leader in all life circumstances. Expect leadership talent, including your own, to emerge in some circumstances and take a back seat in others.

3. Avoid the temptations of the Intensity or Anger Myth. Attempting to motivate others by the force of your temper or other forms of emotional intensity backfires on all concerned.

3

The Roles of Leadership

*For the rest of this century, we shall probably
continue to see a world of business that looks
fundamentally different from the world of the
1950s and 1960s. . . . It will be a world in which
even the best "professional managers" are
ineffective unless they can also lead.*

John Kotter,
The Leadership Factor[6]

A esop tells the story of a dispute between two powerful forces, the sun and the wind. They argued endlessly about which was stronger. To put the matter to a test, the wind picked out a man who was wearing a heavy coat and taking a walk. "To prove I'm stronger than you, I will get that man to remove his coat before you can," boasted the wind. He blew with all his might at the walker. But the harder the wind blew, the tighter the man clung to his coat. Exhausted, the wind offered the sun a try.

The sun cast a pleasant springtime warmth on the man. After a few moments, the man was happy to remove his coat.

In what specific ways do leaders exert their influence over followers and events? The point of Aesop's story is that would-be leaders, or powerful people in general, must have a *variety of techniques and approaches* in their repertoire of leadership skills.

That variety, however, must not be overwhelming if it is to be useful. Listing dozens of leadership activities, for example, would soon prove dizzying to anyone hoping to understand and emulate such behaviors.

Fortunately, the core roles of leadership can be counted on the fingers of one hand—a five-category classification of the central behaviors of leaders-on-the-job. This definition, or taxonomy, of leadership roles may be compared to other lists available in the research literature.[7] Note that the roles discussed in the following pages apply to *all* levels of leadership responsibility in both business and nonbusiness organizations.

THE CORE ROLES OF LEADERS

This overview of leadership roles attempts to include the specific activities that leaders undertake in organizations. The remainder of the book will explain and describe each of these activities, with accompanying suggestions for converting theory into action.

The Vision Role
(Chapters 4, 5, and 6)

Leaders see beyond the events of the moment in the life of their organizations to glimpse what the organization and its membership can become. This vision is rarely the product of otherworldly inspiration, although it may prove inspiring indeed. Instead, the leader's vision is a rational projection or forecast of the organization's best hopes and capabilities.

The vision role is played out through six distinct leadership activities:

- **Vision statements**
  The leader puts his or her vision into
  written and oral form that can be grasped
  by all the organization's stakeholders.

- Visionary actions
  The leader translates visionary words into actions that confirm and support the vision.

- Goal-setting
  The leader sets specific goals that contribute directly to the attainment of the vision.

- Motivation
  The leader encourages organization members to think and act in ways that make the vision an eventual reality.

- Conceptual architecture
  The leader makes sense out of the various aspects and aspirations of the organization's parts. The leader understands and communicates how the various parts of the organization interrelate.

- Prophecy
  Finally, the leader challenges the best talents of group members by making bold pronouncements about problems and opportunities in the organization's near-term or long-term future.

The Relationship Role
(Chapters 7 and 8)

The leader practices and fosters relationships that help the organization achieve its mission. Especially as leaders mature, their value to organizations may lie primarily in the range and depth of their personal and professional associations.

The relationship role can be divided into four areas of leadership activity:

- Teamwork
  The leader assembles and manages teams that make the most of the complementary talents of group members.

- Personnel structures
  The leader establishes the formal relationships among job categories and levels of responsibility within the organization.

- Networks
  The leader initiates or joins networks that prove valuable to the organization.

- Representation
  The leader represents the organization to external stakeholders.

The Control Role
(Chapters 9 and 10)

The leader, usually acting in consultation with others, exercises legitimate control over the organization and its members by defining which of the organization's possible goals will be pursued. In addition, the leader prioritizes the organization's problems and determines resources devoted to their solution.

The control role is enacted in five specific arenas of activity:

- **Problem definition/solution**
  The leader selects which of the organization's problems will be addressed. Although the leader does not usually solve these problems single-handedly, he or she does define what constitutes a solution to a given problem.

- **Decision-making**
  The leader controls the nature and frequency of decision-making in the organization. The leader also determines to what degree others will be involved in the decision-making process.

- **Delegation**
  The leader distributes tasks through delegation and maintains a reporting order among subordinates for the control of these delegated duties.

- **Work descriptions**
  The leader controls the activities of individual organization members by defining the responsibilities and limitations assigned to their positions.

- **Conflict management**
  Through personal intervention and intermediaries, the leader manages and

redirects interpersonal relations that appear
to be out of control.

The Encouragement Role
(Chapters 11 and 12)

The leader establishes a system of rewards and support
that encourages and enables the organization's members. Although money is certainly a strong incentive
for workers, it may often be less important to them than
less tangible rewards and support.

The encouragement role involves three specific
areas of leadership action:

- **Recognition**
  The leader praises individuals and work
  teams who meet or exceed expectations in
  the organization.

- **Reward incentives**
  The leader defines and distributes rewards
  that are meaningful to their recipients.

- **Support**
  The leader devotes part of the
  organization's resources to support the
  work activities of its members.

The Information Role
(Chapters 13 and 14)

Finally, the leader sets up and maintains an information
network that provides both internal and external communication channels.

The information role consists of the following five categories:

- **Communication design**
  The leader oversees the design and maintenance of an information system that serves the needs of the organization in attaining its mission.

- **Monitoring**
  The leader keeps a finger on the pulse of important information sources for early warning of problems and occasions to seize opportunities.

- **Informing**
  The leader provides stakeholders in the organization with the information they need to best serve the organization's interest.

- **Consulting**
  The leader seeks out expert counsel inside and outside the organization.

- **Mentoring**
  The leader encourages learning at all levels within the organization.

Leadership Tips

1. Exercise the *vision role* by words and actions that keep an inspiring, believable future scenario clearly in the minds of organization members.

2. Fulfill the *relationship role* by nurturing teams, networks, and other interpersonal connections that advance the mission of the organization.

3. Use the *control role* not to take all tasks and responsibilities onto yourself, but instead to take charge of the process by which problems are defined, decisions are made, and work is structured.

4. Practice the *encouragement role* by praising, rewarding, and supporting the actions that contribute best to the mission of the organization.

5. Perform the *information role* by making sure that all stakeholders in the organization are "in the loop" through open communication channels.

CHAPTER

4

The Vision Role (1): Statements and Actions

A belief in oneself is the only thing that gives an individual the self-confidence to step into the unknown and to persuade others to go where no one has gone before, but this has to be combined with a decent doubt, the humility to accept that one can be wrong on occasion, that others also have ideas, that listening is as important as talking.

Charles Handy,
in *The Leader of the Future* [8]

L egend has it that a young man stopped on a dusty French path in the late Middle Ages to watch a laborer chipping away pieces from a large stone. "What are you doing?" he asked the worker.

"I'm trying to make this round stone square," came the reply. "I've been working on this one stone for more than a week, and look how little progress I've made."

The young man walked a bit farther and saw another laborer hammering away at a similar block of stone. "What are you doing?" he asked.

The worker replied, "My job. I'm a stone mason."

Not much farther down the path the young man encountered a third laborer, also working a heavy piece of stone. "What are you doing?" he asked.

The worker looked up briefly from his task and replied, "I'm building a cathedral."

———————

Leaders look beyond the immediate problems and projects of their organizations to glimpse what the company and its members can become. What others see as stones, the leader sees as building blocks. What others see as blue sky, the leader sees as blueprints. This is the vision role. For Robert L. Swiggett, Chairperson of the Kollmorgen Corporation, "The leader's job is to create a vision."[9]

Nine visionary corporate leaders were selected by *Esquire* magazine for tribute and analysis. The article began with these words:

> While their contemporaries groped at the present to feel a pulse, or considered the past to discern the course that led to the moment, these nine squinted through the veil of the future. Not that they were mystics. They were much more worldly than that. For most of them, reality was pure and simple; what set them apart was the conviction that a greater reality lay a number of years down the pike.[10]

VISION STATEMENTS

Leaders express, for a given time, the vision of their organizations. At times this statement of vision can be deeply philosophical. One of the best-known vision statements of our century was contained in the "I Have a Dream" speech of Martin Luther King, Jr.:

> This will be the day when all of God's children will be able to sing with new meaning—"my country, 'tis of thee, sweet land of liberty, of thee I sing; land where my fathers died, land of the pilgrim's pride; from every mountainside, let freedom ring"—and if America is to be a great nation, this must become true. . . . And

when we allow freedom to ring . . . we will be able to speed up that day when all of God's children—black and white men, Jews and Gentiles, Protestants and Catholics—will be able to join hands and to sing in the words of the old Negro spiritual: "Free at last, free at last; thank God Almighty, we are free at last."

But *vision,* a word rich in history from association with mystics, poets, and seers, usually has a much more down-to-earth sense when applied to business and other organizations. In our context, *a vision is a relatively brief statement describing broad future aspirations or directions for the organization and some rationale for their pursuit.*

John F. Kennedy presented such a vision to the Congress in announcing, "I think we should go to the moon." Kennedy explained his vision in political as well as scientific terms:

Even though we may not be first in the race to the moon, by rejecting this challenge we are sure to be last.

In keeping with his general management style, Walt Disney issued his initial vision for Disneyland in a statement as clear as a blueprint:

The Main Village, which includes the Railroad Station, is built around a village green or informal park. In the park will be benches, a bandstand, drinking fountains, trees, and shrubs.

It will be a place for people to sit and rest; mothers and grandmothers can watch over small children at play. I want it to be very relaxing, cool and inviting.[11]

For widespread acceptance in the organizations, vision statements must *depart significantly from the status quo* (or else they will not be perceived as visionary) while *not going beyond the general limits of possibility,* as perceived by followers. In other words, a vision statement must be far enough "out" to attract attention, but not so far as to appear crazy or wrongheaded. The vision, in short, must be contagious for all or most members of the group.

Henry M. Boettinger, former director of corporate planning at AT&T, makes the point that "to manage is to lead, and to lead others requires that one enlist the emotions of others to share a vision as their own."[12]

Further, vision statements have more chance of being accepted if the leader takes highly visible, unconventional measures to *support* the vision. According to David E. Berlew, president of Situation Management Systems, Inc., a leader must communicate a vision in a way that "attracts and excites members of the organization."[13] The visionary words that challenge the status quo must be accompanied by *actions* that challenge the status quo.

Substantial research demonstrates that leaders who support their vision statements by risk or self-sacrifice

have a greater chance of having these statements accepted by followers. When leaders appear to be "putting it on the line" in a personal way, followers tend
to take vision statements much more seriously. Socrates'
dictum is still on point: "Know the wise man by the
way he lives."

John Gardner, former Secretary of Health, Education, and Welfare, offers four criteria by which leaders
and their vision statements can be evaluated:

1. Do they release human potential?
2. Do they balance the needs of the individual and the community?
3. Do they defend the fundamental values
   of the community?
4. Do they instill in individuals a sense of
   initiative and responsibility?[14]

Visionary statements that conflict with one or more
of these criteria, Gardner asserts, lead to organizational
failure or organizational immorality, its own form of
failure.

It has recently been argued, in fact, that a leader's
role in larger organizations may be almost exclusively
visionary and symbolic. In *Leaders and the Leadership
Process* (1995), Jon Pierce and John Newstrom ask:

> Does it really make sense to think about lead-
> ership of an entire organization? While it is
> common to hear discussions about the leader-
> ship of such individuals as Jack Welch at General

Electric, Andy Grove at Intel, Bill Gates at Microsoft, Jan Carlzon at Scandinavian Airlines, and Lee Iacocca while he was with Chrysler, observers should question whether these individuals "really made a difference" or whether their role was merely one of being their organization's public figurehead and symbolic leader.[15]

In a similar vein, P. Slater and W. G. Bennis assert in a recent issue of *Harvard Business Review* that "the passing years have . . . given the coup de grace to another force that has retarded democratization—the 'great man' who with brilliance and farsightedness could preside with dictatorial powers as the head of a growing organization."[16]

In other words, it is not enough for a leader to issue a vision statement. The followers must embrace the vision enthusiastically and adopt it as part of the organization's culture. By imparting and sharing the vision, the leader becomes the symbol of the vision itself.

VISIONARY ACTIONS

Perhaps the most stunning visionary action in twentieth-century business occurred when CEO Arthur Houghton, Jr., picked up a lead pipe and summarily smashed more than $100,000 worth of fine crystal. Employees, reporters, radio commentators, stockholders, and the general public got the point loud and clear: Corning was leaving behind the crystal and art glass business with which it had been associated since its purchase of Steuben Glass in 1933.

More recently, Jack Welch, CEO of General Electric, has defended the value of similarly visionary actions that announce radical change in organizations. He compares these actions to sweeping out an old house:

> How would you like to move from a house after 112 years? Think of what would be in the closets and the attic—those shoes that you'll wear to paint next spring, even though you know you'll never paint again. We've got 112 years of closets and attics in this company. We want to flush them out, to start with a brand new house with empty closets, to begin the whole game again.[17]

Initial visionary actions, although dramatic and short-lived, must be followed through with consistency. Subsequent actions need to support and carry out the direction provided by the vision statement. Similar to parenting, leadership involves consistent application of "the rules"; as soon as the actions are perceived as inconsistent with the vision, the vision no longer wields its initial force.

The role of a visionary leader includes several other forms of future-directed actions: *goal-setting* and *motivation,* as described in Chapter Five; and *conceptual architecture* and *prophecy,* as treated in Chapter Six.

Leadership Tips

1. Don't wait for mystic inspiration to state and act upon your vision for your organization. Vision depends more on practical aspiration than transcendent inspiration.

2. Position your vision statement beyond the status quo, but not so far away that it loses credibility.

3. Support your visionary words by visionary actions.

5

The Vision Role (2): Goal-Setting and Motivation

In this business, there are two kinds of people, really: the quick and the dead.

Michael Dell, CEO,
Dell Computer Corporation[18]

In his early days as an entry-level employee at Canon, Inc., Ryuzaburo Kaku made it his practice to "pick out the flaws" in procedures and decisions dictated from top corporate management. "This is something that does not necessarily make one look like a good employee," Kaku recalls.

For a decade, his carefully detailed memos to upper management were uniformly ignored—until the company's financial fortunes took exactly the downward turn that Kaku had predicted. Thereafter his advice was avidly sought, and his vision for the struggling company was taken seriously.

But one vision in particular seemed patently absurd: the notion that Canon could wrest away Xerox's worldwide stranglehold on the photocopier market. Under Kaku's leadership in a variety of company positions culminating at present in chairman of the board, Canon accomplished precisely that.

Although now head of a nineteen-billion-dollar company, Kaku remembers the roots of his vision for the company: "Even in the midst of our biggest changes," he says, "I tried to think from the point of view of an ordinary employee who is thinking of what he or she would do as president."[19]

Ryuzaburo Kaku set important goals for himself in his early days at Canon, and he ended up setting goals for everyone else in the company as well.

GOAL-SETTING

In keeping with his or her vision of the organization's future, the leader *sets and interprets goals* for individuals and work units. These can be as broad as overall achievement targets ("$5,000,000 in sales per quarter") or as specific as "MBOs"—performance objectives agreed to by superior and subordinate. Often the goals refer to market share—"double our market share within two years"—or to specific performance targets or positioning among competitors—"achieve a 25 percent improvement in customer satisfaction ratings" or "surpass Acme in annual sales."

The Management by Objectives (MBO) approach has been particularly popular with American companies since the publication of *The One-Minute Manager* and *In Search of Excellence.* In an MBO system, work goals are negotiated based on five factors:

1. What does the company want done?
2. Within what limits (including time, quality, resources, etc.) must the work be completed?
3. What resources are available for completing the work?
4. How will performance be measured?

5. What is at stake, in terms of visibility, risk, and reputation, in accomplishing the work?

Certainly more than half of Fortune 500 companies, including firms as diverse as Purex, Tenneco, and Black & Decker, now organize work on the basis of negotiated employee objectives. At Cypress Semiconductor, an elaborate computer system tracks progress on each objective to achieve what the company calls a "no-excuses" work environment. Once an objective has been agreed to, either it is met or not met, with rewards or sanctions handed out accordingly.

Other companies have committed themselves to "TQM" (Total Quality Management) goals. At Compaq Computer Corporation (CEO Rod Canion puts a visionary spin on traditional notions of quality control:

> Quality isn't whether or not your products work. Quality is how people do their jobs. Quality is defining your job and then meeting the expectations. When you do that, you raise everyone's consciousness that everything is important. Every piece of the company is important.[20]

The myriad specific goals contained within both the MBO and TQM approaches to goal-setting can become so various that the forest is literally lost among the trees. To keep central goals clearly focused for all employees and stakeholders, some organizations attempt to state their core values or goals in succinct form. Probably one of the most successful of these statements, for its depth, scope, and practicality, is the GE Value Statement (Table 5.1).

Once the goals are widely known within the organization, it is also the leader's function (acting like a Supreme Court) to *interpret those goals.* A prominent business school recently set forth the goal of developing off-site degree programs in Asia and Europe. Needless to say, the school's diverse faculty had widely divergent opinions about the specifics of this initiative: what, where, when, how, and especially how much. It fell to the dean, in his function as visionary leader, to interpret and reinterpret program goals so that they remained within the resource capabilities, personnel abilities, and accreditation realities faced by the school.

Interpretation of goals is akin to pointing out on a map specific roads leading in a desired direction. Robert H. Hayes takes up the analogy:

> When you are lost on a highway, a road map is very useful; but when you are lost in a swamp whose topography is constantly changing, a road map is of little help. A simple compass—which indicates the general direction to be taken and allows you to use your own ingenuity in overcoming various difficulties—is much more valuable.[21]

In short, the ways in which goals are interpreted by the leader depend directly on the circumstances, internal and external, facing the company.

TABLE 5.1
GE VALUE STATEMENT

Business Characteristics

Lean

What: Reduce tasks and the people required to do them.

Why: Critical to developing world cost leadership.

Agile

What: Delayering.

Why: Create fast decision making in rapidly changing world through improved communication and increased individual response.

Creative

What: Development of new ideas—innovation.

Why: Increase customer satisfaction and operating margins through higher value products and services.

Ownership

What: Self-confidence to trust others. Self-confidence to delegate to others the freedom to act while, at the same time, self-confidence to involve higher levels in issues critical to the business and the corporation.

Why: Supports concept of more individual responsibility, capability to act quickly and independently. Should increase job satisfaction and improve understanding of risks and rewards. While delegation is critical, there is a small percentage of high-impact issues that need or require involvement of higher levels within the business and within the corporation.

Reward

What: Recognition and compensation commensurate with risk and performance—highly differentiated by individual, with recognition of total team achievement.

Why: Necessary to attract and motivate the type of individuals required to accomplish GE's objectives. A #1 business should provide #1 people with #1 opportunity.

(Continued)

TABLE 5.1
GE VALUE STATEMENT *(Concluded)*

Individual Characteristics

Reality

What: Describe the environment as it is—not as we hope it to be.

Why: Critical to developing a vision and a winning strategy, and to gaining universal acceptance for their implementation.

Leadership

What: Sustained passion for and commitment to a proactive, shared vision and its implementation.

Why: To rally teams toward achieving a common objective.

Candor/Openness

What: Complete and frequent sharing of information with individuals (appraisals, etc.) and organization (everything).

Why: Critical to employees knowing where they, their efforts, and their business stand.

Simplicity

What: Strive for brevity, clarity, the "elegant, simple solution"—less is better.

Why: Less complexity improves everything, from reduced bureaucracy to better product designs to lower costs.

Integrity

What: Never bend or wink at the truth, and live within both the spirit and letter of the laws of every global business arena.

Why: Critical to gaining the global arenas' acceptance of our right to grow and prosper. Every constituency: shareowners who invest; customers who purchase; community that supports; and employees who depend, expect, and deserve our unequivocal commitment to integrity in every facet of our behavior.

Individual Dignity

What: Respect and leverage the talent and contribution of every individual in both good and bad times.

Why: Teamwork depends on trust, mutual understanding, and the shared belief that the individual will be treated fairly in any environment.

Source: Cited in Warren Bennis, ed., *Leaders on Leadership* (Cambridge, MA: Harvard Business School Press, 1992), p. 27.

MOTIVATION

In addition, the leader acts to energize and direct the efforts of followers through *motivation*. Of the many approaches to motivation, a particularly popular and useful form is *expectancy motivation.*[22] By arousing and sustaining expectations, the leader increases workers' willingness to pursue *goal-directed activities*. In the supermarket business, for example, goal-directed activities for a produce employee might include keeping the fruit and vegetable displays filled and neat, maintaining floors and countertops, and treating customers with personal interest and courtesy.

But why bother? The employee performs these sometimes onerous tasks in order to enjoy *goal-fulfillment activities*. These include receiving an annual bonus based on total produce sales, the respect of other department employees, and praise from the store manager.

As depicted in Figure 5.1, leaders strive to maximize their followers' willingness to concentrate on goal-directed activities rather than eventual rewards. Figure 5.2 represents a group of employees impatient with their day-to-day work, yet eager to participate in the fruits of company success. Figure 5.1, the preferred model for leaders, depicts a group of employees willing to focus their efforts on job tasks, knowing that eventually rewards will be forthcoming.[23]

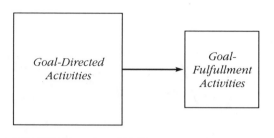

FIGURE 5.1

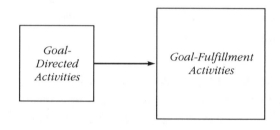

FIGURE 5.2

Leaders should bear in mind, however, the wisdom of McClelland and Atkinson's "50 Percent Curve."[24] Shown in Figure 5.3, it shows how, across industries, workers begin to lose motivation as goal-fulfillment (whether a bonus, award trip, or praise) becomes a sure thing. As might be expected, motivation is also low when goal-fulfillment seems impossible to attain (as, for example, when one employee out of hundreds will be singled out for an award).

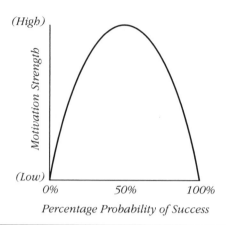

FIGURE 5.3
MOTIVATION IN RELATION TO PROBABILITY OF SUCCESS

The message for leaders in their visionary role is clear: *Keep employee motivation strong by keeping expected rewards attainable but not inevitable.*

Leadership Tips

1. Set and interpret organizational goals, then (often through delegated authority) negotiate specific performance goals with individual employees.

2. Motivate employees by using their own expectations of goal fulfillment and reward.

3. Don't assume that what motivates you also motivates others in your organization.

6

The Vision Role (3): Conceptual Architecture and Prophecy

The leader of the past was a person who knew how to tell. The leader of the future will be a person who knows how to ask.

Peter Drucker

Experienced housepainters often find themselves walking along foot-wide scaffolding planks twenty or more feet off the ground. One foreman tells how he trains apprentice painters to traverse such planks safely. "First, I lay a long plank on the ground and offer the apprentice $5 to walk along it without stepping off. Of course, he or she succeeds and happily accepts the $5. Then I take the same plank to the first-story level of the scaffold, about 10 feet off the ground. Again, I offer $5 if the apprentice will cross the plank safely. When that crossing has been made successfully, I raise the plank to the second-story level, about 20 feet off the ground. Here's where apprentices start to hesitate. They begin to think more about the distance they may fall than about the plank they have safely crossed twice already. My task is to show them how powerful their imaginations can be in determining whether they are confident or fearful on the scaffold. It's always worth my $10 to show them that their safety depends as much on their heads as their legs."

A leader convinces followers that they become what they *think* they will become. If they focus on falling, they will fall. If they focus on walking the plank, they will cross safely.

CONCEPTUAL ARCHITECTURE

More generally, a leader has primary responsibility (though not sole responsibility) for the *conceptual architecture,* or belief systems, within his or her organization. Like a growing tree, an organization is always on its way to *becoming* in the nature and number of its various parts.

A leader imparts to followers an advance approximation or sketch of that organization-to-be as it emerges in the future. For example, a corporate leader often announces efforts to reengineer company processes by pointing out how those processes can be combined, streamlined, or otherwise altered for increased profitability.

Or a leader can suggest additional wings to the central building—perhaps the addition of production facilities for new product lines or the acquisition and integration of other companies. These are all issues of conceptual architecture, for which followers rightly look to their leaders.

Part of that architecture involves feedback systems by which the work force can periodically reflect upon and, if necessary, suggest changes in the corporate vision. Johnson & Johnson periodically assembles selected managers from around the world and instructs them to "get rid of, change, or rededicate themselves" to the company credo.

PROPHECY

Finally, a leader is granted by his or her followers a certain responsibility for *prophecy*. Because the leader occupies a position of relative power, followers attribute to him or her special expertise and insight. They do not demand the kind of substantiation or proof for prophetic statements from the leader that they certainly would demand from one another. When, in the depths of the Great Depression, Franklin Roosevelt rose to proclaim "the only thing we have to fear is fear itself," he was clearly making use of the prophetic rights and privileges granted to him by a frightened, tired populace.

Reliance upon the prophecies of a leader, even when such statements seem irrational, is especially common among followers beset by feelings of alienation, inadequacy, and fear. Hitler's ability to sway millions of listeners by means of raving prophecies can be explained in part (though not excused) by economic depression experienced by his followers in post-World War I Germany.

J. A. Conger, writing in *Organizational Dynamics,* points to the dark side of visionary leadership:

> Though many of these leaders led their organizations on to great successes, others led their organizations on to great failures. The very qualities that distinguish the visionary leader contained the potential for disaster.
>
> Generally speaking, unsuccessful strategic visions can often be traced to the inclusion of

the leaders' personal aims that did not match their constituents' needs. For example, leaders might substitute personal goals for what should be shared goals. They might construct an organizational vision that is essentially a monument to themselves and therefore something quite different from the actual wishes of their organizations or customers.

Moreover, the blind drive to create this very personal vision could result in an inability to see problems and opportunities in the environment. Thomas Edison, for example, so passionately believed in the future of direct electrical current (DC) for urban power grids that he failed to see the more rapid acceptance of alternating power (AC) systems by America's then-emerging utility companies. Thus the company started by Edison to produce DC power stations was soon doomed to failure. He became so enamored of his own ideas that he failed to see competing and, ultimately, more successful ideas.[25]

Mitchell Lee Marks has written recently of CEOs who have reversed leadership mistakes by owning up to their failures. Marks tells the true story of a CEO to whom he has given the fictional name Keith Crowe. This CEO had empowered a team of company employees to undertake a thorough-going redesign of company processes.

After four months of work, involving many late-night and weekend meetings, the day for the presentation arrived. Crowe welcomed the team members to a company conference room, thanked them for their hard work, and expressed his keen interest in hearing their proposals. . . . The team members presented their first and, in their view, most critical recommendation: Overhaul the corporate structure to eliminate barriers to cross-unit cooperation and redundancies in support services and other staff functions.

Crowe exploded: "I did not ask you to redesign the structure of this organization! I asked you to look at work processes and approaches to how people get their jobs done. . . . Why are you distracting us with calls to change the structure?"

The team members' high levels of energy and excitement came tumbling down along with the first reengineering recommendation.

After considerable soul-searching, Crowe reconvened the group for an unusual confession: "I would like to practice what I've been preaching here and admit a couple of mistakes. . . . I have failed miserably, in particular in setting the boundaries. I should have openly communicated any areas that I felt or feel strongly about or that I did not want the teams to address. . . . I failed to do it, and, frankly, I do not have a good reason." [26]

Lee calls the positive company results that followed from Crowe's apology "the power of productive failure. . . . Finding improved ways of getting the job done will occur only if people feel they have permission to fail productively."[27]

Corporate leaders have a chance to have their say, whether through prophecy, explanation, or apology, most obviously in company annual reports. In the "Letter to Stockholders" or similar page, CEOs issue prophecies that stop well short of promises. Phrases such as "bodes well for future quarters," "appears likely to increase total revenues," and "gives reason for optimism for the coming fiscal year" are essentially prophetic in nature. Followers expect such statements from the leader.

If the leader seems to be failing in his or her prophetic role (that is, maintains silence about the future), followers will often demand such statements at news conferences, stockholders' meetings, and other forums. "Where do you see the company going in the next two or three years?" is a common query from followers eager for the sense of security provided by a bold, outspoken leader/prophet. (The line, of course, between prophet and fool has always been tenuous. A leader who makes large claims about the future— claims that come to nothing—rapidly sinks from high to low regard in the eyes of followers.)

The power of prophecy on the part of leaders can often be an influential motivating force for followers. The prophetic claim by school teachers that "you'll need this someday" (for college, career, or other un-named aspects of the future) is intended to keep millions of students somewhat focused on lessons that, in content and pedagogical delivery, would otherwise seem both irrelevant and mind-numbing.

Oscar Wilde's quip, "Nothing succeeds like excess," is apropos in this regard: the predictions of a leader, even when they seem incredible, are believed and acted upon by followers to the extent they feel themselves to be unable or unwilling to participate in the direction of their own fates. The settlement of the American West, for example, was in large part the product of wild prophecies acted upon by desperate immigrants.

Leadership Tips

1. Focus the energy and resolve of organization members by guiding their imagination toward achievable goals.

2. Be the architect of organizational concepts that, taken together, give intellectual shape and direction to the organization.

3. Demonstrate your ability to change directions if necessary as a leader, even when that change involves admission of misjudgment and appropriate apology.

The Relationship Role (1): Teamwork and Personnel Structures

*In the end, all business operations can be
reduced to three words:* people, product,
and profits. *People come first. Unless you've
got a good team, you can't do much with the
other two.*

Lee Iacocca

About 2,600 years ago the Chinese philosopher-poet Lao-Tzu wrote the "Tao Te Ching" or "How Things Work." His words on leadership are timeless:

> The wise leader is like water. Consider water: water cleanses and refreshes all creatures without distinction and without judgment; water freely and fearlessly goes deep beneath the surface of things; water is fluid and responsive; water follows the law freely.
>
> Consider the leader: the leader works in any setting without complaint, with any person or issue that comes on the floor; the leader acts so that all will benefit and serves well regardless of the rate of pay; the leader speaks simply and honestly and intervenes in order to shed light and create harmony.
>
> From watching the movements of water, the leader has learned in action, timing is everything. Like water, the leader is yielding. Because the leader does not push, the group does not resent or resist.

The leader, as Lao-Tzu suggests, is always involved in relationships with others. The nature and quality of those relationships define in large part the success of the leader. These relationships include, in this chapter, the establishment and nurturing of *teamwork* in the organization and the *personnel structures* authorized and supported by the leader. In Chapter Eight we will investigate the types of *networks* encouraged or discouraged by the leader and the forms and occasions of *representation* carried out by leaders at many levels.

TEAMWORK

As described persuasively in such excellent books as *The Wisdom of Teams* (1993), *Team-Based Organizations* (1995), and *Work Teams that Work* (1995), teams in the last decade have revolutionized the way work is accomplished in American corporations. Although there is no single recipe for designing a work team, the following characteristics can generally be observed in successful teams at companies such as Apple Computers, Charles Schwab, AT&T, and General Motors:

- High value is placed on sharing information and group responsibility for problem-solving.
- Power relations (the "pecking order") within the group are downplayed, with an emphasis upon the relative equality of each team member.
- Team spirit and cooperation in meeting or exceeding expectations are encouraged and rewarded.
- Conflict within the team is handled whenever possible by team members themselves.
- Team successes are shared equally by members.

A wealth of research studies show that teams, appropriately structured and managed, bring these significant advantages to organizations across industries: increased worker productivity, more harmonious worker relations, greater loyalty to the organization, less turnover and absenteeism, and increased worker flexibility in adjusting to changing demands and circumstances.[28] There is the additional advantage of having team members cross-trained to fill in for one another as necessary. That broad knowledge of jobs and company processes also puts team members in an excellent position to suggest improvements and cost-saving measures.

But, as many leaders have learned through painful experiment, successful teams are easier to describe than to form. In the words of Pat Carrigan, plant manager at General Motors, "The ability to participate in a challenge and to make it a shared challenge is an incredible task for a leader."[29] Individuals brought together in an organization of any kind do not naturally divide into optimally efficient work teams without the insightful guidance of the organizational leader.

For example, agricultural field hands gathered together on the first day of harvest will typically focus on *task* (what do I have to do?) and *reward* (what will I be paid for doing it?) rather than relationships with fellow workers or efficient ways to work as teams.

Similarly, recruits showing up for "boot camp" in the armed services will cling as long as possible to their natural tendencies to think of "me" before "we." By uniforms, identical haircuts, rote drills and other means, these individualistic tendencies are discouraged in favor of team consciousness. Corporations in the United States, of course, have not embraced these means for building teams. But companies elsewhere, especially in Asia, often do make use of corporate uniforms, drills, and other quasi-militaristic symbols to encourage a firm sense of the team.

Once individuals are melded into an efficient team, productivity can often soar. James M. Kouzes and Barry Z. Posner, in *The Leadership Challenge,* tell a parable-like true story of how a leader supported his team and achieved stunning results:

> An otherwise successful chemical company found that it had a stubborn problem. About 10 percent of all its orders were sent from its loading dock with one sort of defect or another: wrong material, wrong size containers, too much or too little merchandise. A crackdown would bring only a month or two of improvement.
>
> Finally, one enterprising executive decided on a new approach. He knew that in most companies the loading dock team is, at best, lightly regarded. He bet that if the low status of the loading dock workers was turned around, greater productivity would follow. Each member of his team, he decided, would no longer be a worker. He would be a manager. Each would be assigned an account list and would be held responsible for any orders going out to any of his customers.

Suddenly, every shipment that went out had a sponsor, on the dock. It wasn't just the company's shipment anymore. It was a manager's shipment. And each manager cared very much that his order went out without a flaw. Within 90 days, the error rate dropped to two percent. And it has stayed there—or lower—ever since.[30]

The leader's key to forming successful teams lies not in intention (simply wishing teams into existence) but rather in establishing *trust that enables team relationships*. Leaders who are used to trusting primarily in themselves often have difficulty trusting others. Their tendency, instead, is to monitor and control the actions of others—playing, in effect, the puppeteer with strings attached to each individual in the organization. Individuals who have little experience trusting others may often face difficulty in inviting or encouraging trusting relationships in a team environment.

William McGowan, founder of MCI, describes his own struggle to give up some aspects of control for the greater good of team building:

> If you're going to be in a business of any size, you're going to have to develop the kind of leadership qualities that allow you to attract good people, guide them, encourage them, and ultimately trust them—and let them go and do their jobs. Oh, sure, you have to take deep breaths occasionally. But mostly you have to trust them.[31]

PERSONNEL STRUCTURES

Another relationship responsibility of the leader is to establish and support *personnel structures* that help the organization achieve its mission. Among the personnel questions that the leader must answer are the following:

1. Does the leader require an executive team? Who should comprise such a team? From what company constituencies should they be drawn?

2. What hierarchical levels of authority best suit the company's core processes and operations? Should the company be relatively "flat" in layers of authority or "tall"?

3. How should work groups within the company be structured? In what environments will teams be most effective?

4. What personnel procedures and safety nets should be installed to ensure fair play, due process, and appropriate counseling? To whom will employees report workplace problems such as sexual harassment or racial discrimination?

5. What mechanisms should be established to ensure perpetuation of desired personnel structures through recruitment, promotion, and termination procedures? How do you hire the best and keep them?

These questions are not answered by the leader alone, of course. Many decisions are delegated to human resource professionals, legal counsel, and others. But this delegation process still requires a plan and oversight on the part of the organization leader. For general reference in personnel matters, several of the best recent books are listed in the Suggested Reading section.

Leadership Tips

1. Build work teams with careful attention to the characteristics and potential contributions of each member. Don't assume that work teams will form and function effectively on their own.

2. Encourage trust among team members by demonstrating trusting relationships yourself.

3. Give shape to your vision for the organization by the personnel structures you put in place.

8

The Relationship Role (2): Networks and Representation

Leaders are bridges that connect people to the future. They include others' visions in their own, building alliances and partnerships based on shared aspirations.

Caela Farren and Beverly L. Kaye,
founding partners, Career Systems

Max DePree is chairman of Herman Miller, Inc. He explains his central metaphor in his bestselling *Leadership Jazz* (1992):

> I enjoy jazz, and one way to think about leadership is to consider a jazz band. Jazz-band leaders must choose the music, find the right musicians, and perform—in public. But the effect of the performance depends on so many things—the environment, the volunteers playing in the band, the need for everybody to perform as individuals and as a group, the absolute dependence of the leader on the members of the band, the need of the leader for the followers to play well. What a summary of an organization!

DePree is interested in the complex connections present in the professional lives of both jazz musicians and corporate leaders. To extend DePree's analogy, the longer a jazz musician plays with the band, the more music he or she knows. And as a general rule, the higher a leader rises in the organization, the more diverse and valuable his or her network of contacts and associations becomes.

NETWORKS

A leader's network changes both in quality and quantity over time. A mid-level manager in a manufacturing company, for example, could be expected to network occasionally with his or her boss's boss; frequently with fellow managers, steady vendors, and regular customers; and less frequently with competitors, potential clients, and government regulators.

But when that mid-level manager rises to the vice-president level or higher in the organization, his or her network expands (or should expand) dramatically, probably including most of the following contacts:

- Competitors (met through associations and conferences)
- Board members
- Major stockholders
- Legal counsel
- Local, regional, state and federal government officials
- Press representatives
- All levels of executive staff
- Major and potential clients
- Selected employees throughout the organization
- Leaders in allied fields, including business schools
- Product experts and consultants
- Prominent civic and social leaders (perhaps through membership in civic organizations)
- Financial representatives and advisors

At considerable expense in time and resources, leaders cultivate this kind of diverse network for several important reasons. First, the network extends the eyes and ears of the leader to monitor events affecting the organization. A golf game, for example, with a bank president might alert a corporate leader to an impending credit crunch or a window of opportunity for corporate borrowing.

Second, the network extends the leader's hands in reaching out for assistance, from friends and perhaps "friends of friends"—politicians, lawyers, real estate brokers, trainers, journalists, and so forth. These various contacts can often provide direct assistance in resolving company problems, or at least can serve as conduits of valuable information about how such problems can be addressed.

Finally, without overextending the analogy, it can be said that the network extends the leader's heart. He or she learns through community contacts to perceive business in its social and ethical dimensions. The leader's membership in the local Rotary Club, for example, may draw the company into partnership with others in sponsoring charitable projects, local athletic teams, and scholarship programs.

A leader's common touch in human relationships pays extraordinary dividends in terms of respect and loyalty from followers. Retired Congressional Representative Norman Shumway (R-California) recalls the following example of the "human touch":

I happened to have two of my sons with me in my office. My sons were high school age at the time. We were leaving the office to go to the parking lot which was under my building.

The entrance to the House Gymnasium is right there, and we noticed three or four Secret Service vehicles down in the parking lot. So I thought, "Well, George Bush [who was the vice president] must be in there playing racquetball." So I said to my boys, "Come on, you can watch him play." I took my sons in, and by the time we got there he had gone to take a shower and was getting dressed by his locker. So I walked into the locker room, and there was George, standing by himself, in front of his locker, with shorts on. I said, "Mr. Vice President, I'd like you to meet two of my sons." And he said, "Oh, Norm! How are you doing?"

He stood there talking to them for about ten minutes, with all this water dripping off of him. Here's the second most important man in America talking to these teenage boys as if they were his own children. He was really down-to-earth that way, and I like that about him.[32]

A Chinese proverb states that "if you want one year of prosperity, grow grain; if you want ten years of prosperity, grow trees; if you want one hundred years of prosperity, grow people." Networks are the fertile ground for "growing" people who can be crucial to the success of your organization.

Leaders can nurture their network relationships in at least four ways:

1. *Have something to trade.* Networks among leaders are in part a trading system for information, contacts, and favors. A leader enhances his or her value within a network by having something of value to offer others.

2. *Avoid explicit quid pro quo favors.* Friendly relationships with network members are best established and maintained by favors without "strings attached." Network members should never be led to feel that your actions are predicated simply on what's in it for you.

3. *Seek out groups that offer useful contacts.* Social clubs, civic organizations, political committees, professional organizations, advisory boards, and alumni groups all offer congenial ways to meet new members of your expanding network.

4. *Maintain your contact with network members.* An occasional telephone call, e-mail message, card, or personal visit keeps network members aware of your friendship, interests, and needs. At the same time, you keep yourself apprised of events, changes, and relationships within the network.

As a leader's career matures, his or her network often becomes a highly valued asset for the leader's organization or for the leader himself or herself in changing jobs. Aerospace companies, for example, are notorious for hiring retired generals and admirals as high-paid consultants able to use their personal networks to advantage in promoting company contracts.

REPRESENTATION

The leader also determines where and how to represent the organization. The leader must decide, for example, if he or she should appear in person on company television commercials. Which speaking engagements should the leader accept? To what petitions, letters, or organizations should the leader lend his or her name and sponsorship? Which meetings should the leader actually lead, and which should he or she delegate to others? What company, social, or civic events require the leader's presence and visibility?

These questions and more must, of course, be answered case by case, with an eye toward what is potentially to be gained or lost. In any case, the leader can be sure that every aspect of his or her physical and emotional presentation of self will be interpreted at least in part by others as a reflection upon (or characterization of) the leader's organization.

This attribution process obeys few rules of political correctness. An elderly leader, especially one whose voice and hearing are somewhat impaired, may unfortunately lead some to draw unfavorable conclusions about that leader's organization. A leader in the grip of speaker's nerves during a presentation may inadvertently shake the confidence of the organization's stakeholders. A misconceived or ill-timed comment or joke told by a leader during a television or radio appearance can undo dozens of company advertisements.

At a minimum, leaders owe their organizations faithful adherence to four principles of effective representations:

1. *Speak well.* A leader must master the rudiments of effective public speaking, especially for the purposes of luncheon addresses, introductions, briefings, and short speeches of appreciation. Toastmasters organizations can be particularly helpful for leaders who need practice and coaching in giving effective oral presentations.

2. *Handle questions well.* Leaders are judged as much by their spontaneous moments in answering questions from the audience, media representatives, and community members as by their skills in making formal presentations.

3. *Look the part.* Mercifully, there is no "dress for success" guide for organizational leaders. But common sense suggests that the leader assess his or her physical appearance, dress, and demeanor in relation to audience expectations.

4. *Relate well.* Leaders are judged in part by how they seem to relate to those around them. A standoffish leader who seems to be shunned by others in a meeting, press conference, or other venue will inevitably arouse negative judgments, no matter what he or she has to say.

Leadership Tips

1. Try each day to extend and deepen relationships that may be useful to your organization.

2. Recognize that the nature of your relationships and networks will change as you rise as a leader in the organization. Make the most of new opportunities for relationships made possible by your new levels of responsibility and prominence.

3. Evaluate as objectively as possible your strengths and weaknesses as a public representative for your organization. Polish your representation skills, particularly those related to public speaking, handling questions, leadership image, and relationship abilities.

9

The Control Role (1): Problem Definition/ Solution and Decision-making

The three major challenges CEOs will face have little to do with managing the enterprise's tangible assets and everything to do with monitoring the quality of leadership, the work force, and relationships.

Frances Hesselbein,
former chief executive officer,
Girl Scouts of the U.S.A.[33]

Steven Jobs, founder of Apple Computer, had tried virtually everything to attract David Sculley (then CEO of PepsiCo) to the chief executive position at Apple. Over a period of weeks, Sculley had turned down mammoth salary offers and lucrative stock considerations from Apple.

As a last gambit, Jobs flew to meet with Sculley. Jobs spoke passionately about the global promise of personal computing and Apple's prominent role in that future. He then paused and, with obvious reference to Pepsi, said to Sculley: "Do you really want to sell brown sugar-water the rest of your life?" Sculley took the helm at Apple and oversaw its best years of meteoric growth.

———————

Leaders exercise influence over others by selecting and acting upon problems that matter. For David Sculley, money was not the primary issue in deciding upon a major career change. What mattered, as Jobs knew, was playing a significant role in a revolutionary cultural and technological change. In his years as Apple's CEO, Sculley would exercise control in much the same way that Jobs influenced him to join Apple in the first place: by getting directly to the issues that mattered most for employees. It was his special talent to pose important problems for bright employees who craved creative involvement in problem-solving.

CONTROL

Especially in the light of current thinking urging increased employee empowerment and more widely distributed decision-making, the concept of *control* may rest uncomfortably at first with a leader. Some leaders do not want to position themselves as control figures within the organization, and others simply feel that most organizational processes are beyond their individual control.

This resistance to the control role can be found in the full range of organizations, from business to politics. As a corporation grows in size, "control" on the part of the CEO may be more a fond illusion than a workday reality. As Abraham Lincoln said in the throes of the Civil War, "I am more controlled by events than I control them."

Some leaders regret loss of control and try to maintain a firm grasp on the reins of power as long as possible. Other leaders seek a form of backstage control in which they can influence the course of events in their organizations without overtly controlling the actions of their employees.

This chapter emphasizes ways in which leaders can exert control *through* people rather than *upon* them. Social psychologist David McClelland advises that "if a leader wants to have far-reaching influence, he [or she] must make his followers feel powerful and able to accomplish things on their own. . . . Even the most dictatorial leader does not succeed if he has not in-stilled in at least some of his followers a sense of power and the strength to pursue the goals he has set."[34]

Jack Welch, chairman and CEO of General Elec-tric, foresees the importance of the passionate leader who empowers others:

> The world of the '90s and beyond will not belong to "managers" or those who make the numbers dance, as we used to say, or those who are conversant with all the business jargon we use to sound smart. The world will belong to passionate, driven "leaders"—people who not only have an enormous amount of energy, but who can energize those whom they lead.[35]

Such leaders are able to maintain a firm sense of control, even when the organization faces internal or external crisis. The organizational leader defines and prioritizes problems, as well as approaches to their solution; controls *decisions* that are made, and how they are made; supervises *delegation* and its manage-ment; oversees *work descriptions,* as developed infor-mally within the organization and formally in job descriptions; and provides for *conflict management* within the organization.

Problem Definition and Solution

Of the hundreds of problems faced daily by any or-ganization of even moderate size, the leader plays a key role in selecting those problems that will be given attention, in terms of human and financial resources. This vital control function on the part of the leader is usually conducted consultatively, of course. But leaders inevitably find themselves having to choose among many pressing problems, any one of which could legitimately occupy the best efforts of the organization. How does a leader decide which problems matter most?

Many leaders make use of the "Left Unsolved . . ." technique to settle in their own minds those problems that require immediate surgery, those that require a bandage, and those that can be postponed with an aspirin or less. The technique works as follows. Insert a short statement of the problem in the blank for each of the following questions. By jotting down your thoughts for each question, you apprise yourself more fully of the nature, magnitude, and urgency of the problem.

Left Unsolved . . .

1. This problem would impact people or groups in this order:

   _____

   _____

2. This problem would prevent the company from these desired actions:

   _____

   _____

3. This problem is (increasing/decreasing) in severity due to the following factors:

_____

_____

4. This problem can be divided in these subparts:

_____

_____

5. This problem will produce the following related problems:

_____

_____

Note that this brief rubric does not attempt to evaluate causes or assess blame for the problem (although those topics surely must be included in any approach to a workable solution). The "Left Unsolved . . ." technique directs the leader's attention to the nature, impact, and ramifications of the problem. These are the considerations that must be uppermost in deciding which problems deserve attention first in an environment with limited resources for problem-solving.

For example, consider four well-known problems faced daily at a local post office branch:

1. Two carriers have been receiving angry complaints from people on their routes for a variety of alleged offenses, including putting mail in the wrong

mailboxes, abusing neighborhood pets, and leaving gates open.

2. A patron claims that the post office has somehow lost a certified letter containing a cashier's check for several thousand dollars.

3. The air conditioning is malfunctioning in the mail sorting room, causing a significant work slowdown among sweltering employees.

4. The Regional Director of the U.S. Post Office sends a fax to remind the local postmaster to file employee diversity certification forms no later than the deadline, two days hence.

Using the "Left Unsolved . . ." questions, the postmaster decides to prioritize problems in the following way. The diversity forms are dispatched first, not only because the postmaster is under a legal obligation to do so but also because a deadline looms and the forms can be handled quickly. The air-conditioning problem is tackled next, because it threatens the health and efficiency of the work force. The complaints against the two carriers are next in priority, because a significant number of patrons are affected. Finally, the missing certified letter gets attention; it involves only one patron, and its solution will probably require a search of several postal facilities.

By controlling the type of problem selected for attention by the organization, the leader maintains control over the human resources and budget of the organization.

Decision-making

Leaders make the key decisions by which organizations rise or fall—and for which leaders themselves are praised or blamed. Few organizations are so autocratic, of course, as to tolerate for long a leader who makes major decisions without consulting a wide range of stakeholders and knowledgeable employees.

From the leader's point of view, a tightrope of sorts must be traversed in making decisions expeditiously while including the input of others. As David McClelland writes:

> How much initiative he should take, how persuasive he should attempt to be, and at what point his clear enthusiasm for certain goals becomes personal authoritarian insistence that those goals are the right ones whatever the members of the group may think, are all questions calculated to frustrate the well-intentioned leader. If he takes no initiative, he is no leader. If he takes too much, he becomes a dictator, particularly if he tries to curtail the process by which members of the group participate in shaping group goals.[36]

To resolve this leadership bind, some leaders make the mistake, consciously or unconsciously, of surrounding themselves with men and women who can be counted on to agree with the leader's position. Social psychologist Irving Janis studied this tendency at length. When a group of individuals lose their individual evaluative abilities, Janis says, they are in the grip of "GroupThink."[37]

The members' motives for joining in GroupThink may be varied. Some members may "go along" with ideas with which they disagree because they cherish the harmony of the group or fear the repercussions of disharmony in the group. Others may participate in GroupThink out of blind or calculated loyalty to the leader (who, in this case, has indicated to the group what its opinion should be).

Certain symptoms tell a leader when his or her executive committee, quality circle, or other decision-support group is falling prey to GroupThink. This enemy to sound decision-making is probably present when group members believe any of the following:

- No one can or should resist the expressed will of the group.
- Data in conflict with group opinion and information must, by definition, be incorrect.
- The group is incapable of doing the wrong thing from an ethical or moral standpoint.
- Nongroup competitors are stupid, uninformed, and weak.
- All group members should have as their primary goal to support one position.
- If a member has private reservations about an idea, it's best not to mention it.
- There's little need to discuss topics thoroughly, since the group will probably reach quick agreement.

• Information conflicting with group positions isn't worth hearing.

Janis points to the Bay of Pigs fiasco during the
Kennedy administration as a prime example of
GroupThink:

> The group that deliberated on the Bay of Pigs
> decision included men of considerable talent.
> Like the President, all of the main advisors
> were shrewd thinkers, capable of objective
> rational analysis, and accustomed to speaking
> their minds. But collectively they failed to detect
> the serious flaws in the invasion plan.[38]

That plan involved amazing naïveté by hindsight
(as many of the original group members have since
written). The plan involved sending no more than 1,400
Cuban exiles as a catalyst force intended to motivate
the Cuban people to join this small band and overthrow
Castro. Just the opposite occurred: the small force was
beaten into hasty retreat, Cubans committed even more
strongly to programs of their leader, and the Soviets
took advantage to place troops and nuclear missiles
less than 90 miles from United States shores.

The clear alternative to GroupThink is a decision-
making environment in which every contributor to the
decision feels obligated to give his or her best judgment, no matter if it conflicts with the "party line" or
wishes of the leader. Leaders can encourage this kind
of decision-support network by (a) listening attentively

to all points of view; (b) praising or otherwise reward-ing all whose insights contributed to the decision, including those critical of the decision itself; and (c) educating the decision-support group on the impor-tance of ongoing diversity in opinion and viewpoint.

Even after a leader has received the best counsel of the best minds, he or she still faces risk and un-certainty in making decisions. Tom Peters and Bob Waterman, in their book *In Search of Excellence,* advise a somewhat insouciant attitude that blends courage and curiosity: "Do it. Fix it. Try it." Leaders who aren't afraid of occasional missteps give themselves permission to make bold decisions. In the great majority of cases, wrong decisions can be corrected ("fix it"), and a new course can be plotted toward success ("try it").

Leadership Tips

1. Exert control *through* people, not *upon* them.

2. Exercise control by your selection of organizational issues for attention. Avoid being manipulated by issues selected and defined by others.

3. Beware of GroupThink among subordinates by encouraging the free expression of opinions.

10

The Control Role (2): Delegation, Work Descriptions, and Conflict Management

Will the leader please stand up? Not the president,
or the person with the most distinguished title,
but the role model. Not the highest paid person in
the group, but the risk taker. . . . Not the taker,
but the giver. Not the talker, but the listener.

C. William Pollard, Chairman,
The ServiceMaster Company[39]

In the early years of this century, a journalist named Napoleon Hill was given the assignment of interviewing steel magnate Andrew Carnegie. Their conversation proved momentous for Hill. Carnegie not only revealed to Hill the secrets of his own success, but also convinced Hill to undertake what would turn out to be a twenty-year investigation of successful people. Over the years he conducted in-depth interviews with Theodore Roosevelt, Henry Ford, Thomas Edison, George Eastman, John D. Rockefeller, Clarence Darrow, and scores of other notables.

Hill concluded that none of his interviewees was truly "self-made." All had relied upon the talents and goodwill of those they originally worked for and those who later worked with them and for them. Carnegie's own tombstone conveyed the heart of Hill's research in one succinct sentence: "Here lies one who knew how to get around him men who were cleverer than himself."

———

Wise leaders learn early in their careers to maximize their influence on any given project by inviting the participation of talented subordinates. The art of leadership, in fact, has been described by some corporate leaders as the process of turning one's work over to others.

DELEGATION

Leaders exercise organizational control in determining when, how, and to whom responsibilities are to be delegated. It is not uncommon, of course, for some leaders to resist delegation. Particularly in start-up companies, the original company leader may maintain hands-on, micromanagerial control over company processes and procedures much longer than is good for the company's or the leader's health. In a word, these leaders fear delegation, and they have forgotten Emerson's advice to "always do what you are afraid to do."

Other leaders hesitate to delegate because they consider the training, oversight, and performance evaluation process for subordinates more onerous than simply doing the job themselves. These are the rugged individualists of industry and commerce who pride themselves on accomplishing Herculean tasks, maintaining a mind-numbing work schedule, and foregoing the breaks and vacations taken by others in their organization. They seldom provide for transition planning; when they eventually leave their positions (often feet first), no one is prepared to step into their shoes. While this fact may be taken as a tribute to the hard work of the individual, it is simultaneously the death knell of many organizations that can't carry on without their know-all, do-all leader.

But in most organizations leaders must delegate to survive as individuals and for the organization to thrive. By delegating, a leader increases the quality and speed with which decisions are made, particularly in cases where the subordinate to whom a task is delegated knows more about the matter at hand than the leader. In rapidly changing business environments, this distributed form of decision-making can help an organization respond successfully to emerging opportunities, in the same way that parallel processing computing allows greater programming flexibility and processing power.

In addition, appropriate delegation frees busy leaders to spend their time on more important matters, while passing on less important tasks to subordinates. Leaders who claim (often rightly) that they could do given tasks faster and better than subordinates fail to take into consideration the work they *cannot* take on because of the plethora of everyday tasks they face. Companies don't want leadership time spent on tasks that could be accomplished just as well by others.

Delegation also pays dividends to the organization by training subordinates to assume more and more important responsibility. Employees who have matured through such delegation are more ready to assume leadership responsibilities themselves in the organization. Until that time, they are more likely to feel satisfaction with their jobs because they have been trusted with increasing levels of responsibility. This increased level of satisfaction often prevents employees from seeking work elsewhere, saving the company the considerable expense of recruitment and training.

Leaders also control the type and amount of responsibility they transfer to subordinates through delegation. The most common form of delegation is the new task/new authority package. For example, a subordinate may be given the new task of coordinating new product approvals with government regulators. The new authority that comes with that task is the ability to make changes (perhaps in product configuration or ingredients) as required by the regulators.

Alternatively, the leader may assign limited authority to accompany a delegated new task. A negotiator in the company, for example, may be given an important contract to negotiate, but his or her authority to bargain may be limited in several areas. The leader of the organization may want to reserve final say on matters such as profit margins, deadlines, and contingencies.

The ultimate form of delegation, perhaps, exists in the relation between a coach and the team in professional sports. In this case, the coach is entirely off the field of play; all action must be carried forth by the players to whom he has delegated responsibilities. What distinguishes successful delegation from unsuccessful delegation in this environment is the coach's grasp of desired outcomes—and his or her ability to communicate those outcomes to the players.

The legendary football coach Vince Lombardi explained the difference between a good coach and a bad coach in this way:

> The best coaches know what the end result looks like, whether it's an offensive play, a defensive play, a defensive coverage, or just some area of the organization. If you don't

know what the end result is supposed to look like, you can't get there. All the team basically do the same things. We all have drafts, we all have training camps, we all have practices. But the bad coaches don't know what the hell they want. The good coaches do.[40]

In delegating tasks, the leader must decide the extent to which a subordinate must "check in" for approval or guidance. At the lowest level of delegation, a subordinate checks with the boss whenever a difficulty or unexpected event occurs. At a somewhat higher level, the subordinate may be given authority to make the decision about how to handle problems, so long as approval is given by the leader prior to the implementation of those decisions. Finally, at the highest level of delegation, the subordinate makes decisions and implements them without prior approval by the leader of the organization.

Although delegation often depends on the personalities and situations in given circumstances, the following guidelines can help leaders strategize on what to delegate, when, and to whom:

1. *Delegate tasks in such a way that they fit in with the subordinate's career path.* Delegation, after all, is a training function as well as an expediency. For example, an outstanding sales representative could be delegated the task of reviewing and recommending sales seminars to be taken by others in the sales force. In this way, the outstanding rep learns new ideas and skills for future management responsibilities.

2. *Mix hard, easy, long, and quick tasks in delegating to subordinates.* In too many companies, employees associate delegation with drudgery, largely because the boss off-loads on them only the unpleasant, time-consuming tasks. Although these tasks will always be part of business realities, leaders should be mindful— even to the point of keeping notes—of which employees have gotten the short end of the delegation stick lately.

3. *Specify responsibilities, reporting requirements, and performance measures clearly.* In the rush to pass along urgent tasks to others, leaders sometimes project their own years of experience (which they have come to call "common sense") onto subordinates. For the purposes of effective delegation, it is almost impossible to be too clear when telling a subordinate exactly what you wish done, how and when the subordinate is to report progress or problems, and how you will determine how well the job is being done.

4. *Support the subordinate with the same or greater resources that you would provide for yourself in accomplishing the task.* Leaders who have grown accustomed to power, influence, and contacts in an organization sometimes fail to understand why a subordinate can't navigate corporate waters as quickly as they in accomplishing a task. Leaders must consider what information, authority contacts, support personnel, equipment, and funding the subordinate will require in fulfilling the delegated responsibility.

WORK DESCRIPTIONS

The leader also exercises control by influencing the way work is segmented and described. In establishing his renowned assembly lines, Henry Ford demonstrated his control as a leader not so much by his interaction with employees as by his initial architectural activity in setting forth position descriptions. Once finalized on paper as a "job description," the conceptual framework of an employee's actions (as well as the boundaries of the employee's responsibilities) becomes a powerful controlling force for company hiring, training, performance evaluation, and promotion.

Work descriptions can focus on tasks, relationships, or both. The following job description (somewhat typical of an entry-level position) attempts to define specific tasks for which the employee will be held accountable.

In the next job description, however, the focus is clearly on relationships that the employee must nurture and support. This job description is more characteristic of upper management positions. Whatever tasks come with the job will emerge through these relationships and perhaps cannot be stated in advance with any precision.

Many leaders involved in reengineering efforts find that they exercise control over the new "shape" of the organization most potently by the way they influence the description of work positions.

BREVARD GENERAL HOSPITAL
Job Description

Job Title:	Job Analyst	**Job Code:**	166.088
Date:	January 3, 1996	**Author:**	John Doakes
Job Location:	Personnel Department	**Job Grade:**	
Supervisor:	Harold Grantinni	**Status:**	Exempt

Job Summary: Collects and develops job analysis information through interviews, questionnaires, observation, or other means. Provides other personnel specialists with needed information.

Job Duties: Designs job analysis schedules and questionnaires. Collects job information.

Interacts with workers, supervisors, and peers.

Writes job descriptions and job specifications.

Reports safety hazards to area manager and safety departments.

Verifies all information through two sources.

Performs other duties as assigned by supervisors.

Working Conditions: Works most of the time in well-ventilated modern office. Data collection often requires on-site work under every working condition found in company. Works standard 8 A.M. to 5 P.M. except to collect second-shift data and when traveling (one to three days per month).

The above information is correct as approved by:

(Signed) _____   (Signed) _____
       Job Analyst   Department Manager

BREVARD GENERAL HOSPITAL
Job Description

Job Title:	Job Analyst	**Job Code:**	166.088
Date:	January 3, 1996	**Author:**	John Doakes
Job Location:	Personnel Department	**Job Grade:**	
Supervisor:	Harold Grantinni	**Status:**	Exempt

Skill Factors

Education: College degree required.

Experience: At least one year as job analyst trainee, recruiter, or other professional assignment in personnel area.

Communication: Oral and written skills should evidence ability to encapsulate job data succinctly. Must be able to communicate effectively with diverse work force, including foreign-born employees.

Effort Factors

Physical demands: Limited to those normally associated with clerical jobs: sitting, standing, and walking.

Mental demands: Extended visual attention is needed to observe jobs. Initiative and ingenuity are mandatory since job receives only general supervision. Judgment must be exercised on job features to be emphasized, jobs to be studied, and methods used to collect job data. Decision-making discretion is frequent. Analyzes and synthesizes large amounts of abstract information into job descriptions, job specifications, and job standards.

Working Conditions
Travels to hospital clinics in county from one to three days per month. Travels around each work site collecting job information. Works mostly in an office setting.

Conflict Management

Without putting too much weight on the metaphor, a leader in an organization can be said to perform a parental role of sorts in controlling conflict among organizational members. Some leaders (often to their disappointment) make an effort to banish conflict altogether. They communicate to their work force that the "happy family" tolerates no conflict. Disagreements over policy, procedures, or business strategies are all swept aside in the name of good fellow feelings.

More mature leaders recognize that conflict is an inevitable part of any lively organization and portends an intellectually challenging and honest work environment. In the language of sailing, these managers don't fear gusts of conflict; instead, they interpret such energy as a chance to break away from the pack, to gain speed, to change directions.

Uncontrolled conflict, of course, destroys the organization. The leader must be able to read signs of interpersonal and intergroup conflict accurately, then go on to channel that conflict constructively in service of the organization's mission.

In this sense, the organization's leader controls conflict by monitoring it closely. The following signs are particularly important in spotting when conflict is brewing:

- Too much strong feeling attached to seemingly trivial topics

- Rapidly shifting eyes or glaring in interpersonal contacts
- Name-calling and personal attacks
- Implied or expressed threats
- Expressions of despair, anger, panic, or desperation
- Needless harping on the same point
- Obvious efforts to gather allies and set up opposed camps on an issue
- Inappropriate use of biting humor and sarcasm
- Obvious moves to isolate some individuals[41]

Just as important for a leader to recognize are the signs that group members are sidestepping potential conflict:

- Unwillingness to discuss anything except "safe" topics
- Premature agreement just to "keep the peace"
- Perpetually letting others carry the ball
- Silence from usually talkative group members
- Failure to move on to the next logical steps
- Unwillingness to share information and opinions

- Knowing glances and nonverbal cues
- Recycling of old ideas[42]

Leaders can monitor conflict best by active listening. This higher level of listening requires more involvement and energy than casual listening (to a radio in the background), social listening (to a friend's story at a party), or attentive listening (to a lecture or sermon). Active listening requires that the leader adopt what Carl Rogers calls "an empathic attitude"—a willingness to listen thoroughly to the many levels of messages at hand. Consider some of these levels:

- *The occasion for the message.* Why is the person contacting me now?
- *The length of the message.* What can length or brevity reveal about the importance of the message to the person?
- *The words chosen.* Is the message communicated in formal, aloof language? Impatient slang?
- *The volume and pace.* What can these tell me about the emotional pressure behind the message?
- *The pauses and hesitations.* How do these add meaning to the main message?
- *The nonverbal cues.* What can eye contact, posture, facial expression, and gestures tell me about the message?

David Burns, M.D., explains the technique of active, empathetic listening in this way: "The key is to put yourself in the other person's shoes and look for the truth in what that person is saying."[43] But Dr. Burns admits that active listening isn't always easy. He tells of a recent listening challenge of his own:

> I was counseling a businessman named Frank who tends to be overbearing when he's upset. Frank told me that I was too preoccupied with money and that he shouldn't have to pay at each of our sessions. He wanted to be billed monthly.
>
> I felt annoyed because it seemed that Frank always had to have things his way. I explained that I had tried monthly billing, but it hadn't worked out because some patients didn't pay. Frank argued that he had impeccable credit and knew much more about credit and billing than I did.
>
> Suddenly I realized I was missing Frank's point. "You're right," I said. "I'm being defensive. We should focus on the problems in your life and not worry so much about the money."
>
> Frank immediately softened and began talking about what was really bothering him, which were some personal problems. The next time we met, he handed me a check for twenty sessions in advance.[44]

Through the kind of self-giving, interested listening Dr. Burns describes, leaders can come to know the nature and degree of conflict active in their organizations and thereby position themselves to control it more effectively.

Leaders must come to terms with their own attitudes and intentions regarding the exercise of control in their organizations. No matter whether the leaders decide to exert control from behind the scenes or in an overt, micromanagerial way, they must avoid GroupThink on the part of their advisors and employees. Leaders should solicit opinions from others in a penalty-free environment that encourages honesty, even when such opinions are diametrically opposed to the leader's position.

One often overlooked aspect of control is the selection initiative of leaders, as they choose issues for attention in the organization. Leaders can be proactive in defining these issues rather than reactive to issues defined by others in the organization.

Some leaders, particularly in start-up organizations, resist delegation in a wrong-headed attempt to "do it all." Properly viewed, delegation is not a loss of control, but instead an extension of control. Such delegation can be formalized in well-drawn work descriptions, which define employee interactions and relations with management.

Finally, leaders must accept a degree of conflict as the sign of a healthy, growing organization. Such conflict should be monitored for extremes so that it does not reach unproductive levels or is not unnecessarily suppressed and avoided.

Leadership Tips

1. Delegate to extend your control, not to dilute it, particularly in well-drawn work descriptions.

2. Accept a degree of conflict as the inevitable sign of a vibrant, learning organization.

3. Develop personal and organizational sensing mechanisms for monitoring conflict levels.

4. Use active listening to understand organizational conflict and to channel it constructively.

11

The Encouragement Role (1): Recognition and Reward Incentives

I believe that you should praise people whenever you can; it causes them to respond as a thirsty plant responds to water.

Mary Kay Ash, Founder,
Mary Kay Cosmetics.

C William Pollard, chairman of The ServiceMaster Corporation, tells the parable-like true story of two workers he observed in his business travels:

> During a trip to Leningrad in 1989, I met a custodian named Olga. She had the job of mopping a lobby floor in a large hotel. I took an interest in her and her task and engaged her in conversation. Olga had been given a "T" frame for a mop, a dirty rag, and a dirty bucket of water to do her job. She wasn't really cleaning the floor; she was just moving dirt from one section to another. . . . Olga was not proud of what she was doing. . . . She was lost in a system that did not care. . . .
>
> By contrast, I had an experience just a few days later while visiting a hospital that ServiceMaster serves in London, England. As I was introduced to one of the housekeepers as the chairman of ServiceMaster, she put her arms around me and gave me a big hug. She thanked me for the training and tools she had received to do her job. She then showed me all that she had accomplished in cleaning patient rooms, providing a detailed "before and after" ServiceMaster description. She was proud of her work. She had bought into the result because someone had cared enough to show her the way and recognize her efforts when the task was done. She was looking forward to the next accomplishment.[45]

Pollard draws deep satisfaction out of helping to create *internal* wealth for his employees in the form of dignity, skill, and pride in accomplishments.

Leaders like Pollard are simultaneously the creators and central conduits for a broad range of rewards and support activities directed toward group members. Among the many forms that rewards can take are *recognition* (by individuals and groups) and *incentives* (including pay, promotion, travel, benefits, and a broad range of "perks"). *Support* activities on the part of the leader include environmental provisions, necessary equipment, training, information access, and other measures that sustain and further an employee's efforts. (Support activities are discussed in Chapter 12.)

Certainly one of the least ambiguous definitions of leadership was that of Vance Packard in *The Pyramid Climbers:* "In essence leadership appears to be the art of getting others to want to do something you are convinced should be done."[46] By getting others to *want* to act, rewards in all their forms have profound effects upon the organization and its members. Appropriately conceived and timed, rewards can increase and sustain employee motivation, clarify which work behaviors are desired from employees, increase job satisfaction and thereby lessen turnover and absenteeism, and make it easier for the organization to attract outside talent through recruitment.

RECOGNITION

One of the least expensive, yet most effective ways to take note of achievement and motivate future efforts on the part of an employee is to recognize the employee's achievement, usually in a public way. This form of reward is particularly useful for leaders whose hands are tied (often by labor contracts, limited resources, or constrained authority) and who cannot give meaningful cash bonuses, vacation awards, and other tangible rewards. Recognition can take the form of a certificate, pin, or other symbolic award; an oral or written encomium, preferably delivered in public; and increased attention in some other visible way to the person's achievements, perhaps through displays of his or her work, "employee of the month" selection, or parking-space perks for a period.

Recognition is distinguished from other forms of rewards by its relative lack of cash value; recognition targets the ego, not the wallet, of the recipient.

Several conditions must exist for recognition to be significant as a reward and motivator in the eyes of the recipient and the observing group. First, the recognition must come as a result of some measured accomplishment known by the group. In other words, recognition by the lottery system would not be taken as a compliment to one's efforts or as a strong incentive to perform in the future. Second, the recognition must come from a respected authority figure in the organization, usually someone with substantial power over the future career path of the recipient and many others in the organization.

Recognition from a consultant, no matter what his or her academic degrees and experience, would probably be much less meaningful to an employee than recognition from his or her boss or, better yet, that boss's boss. Recognition from one's peers can be appreciated and is often a significant motivator for continued or increased excellence in performance.

Third, recognition is most effective when it comes with no strings attached. An employee would naturally feel some ambivalence in receiving an award certificate for past accomplishments on the condition that he or she exceeds quota in the coming year. Finally, recognition may come as a recurring periodic event in an organization (for example, the annual Secretary of the Year award) or as in a non-periodic way, with recognition doled out, often as a surprise, immediately after particular work goals are achieved by an individual or group.

REWARD INCENTIVES

Reward incentives are more tangible and take the form of bonuses, pay increases, more prestigious assignments, better schedules, more desirable work space, award trips, new cars, and other attractive motivators. In the parlance of an old business cliché, "What gets rewarded gets done."

Most motivators are given or at least promised at the outset of effort as an inducement to eventual achievement. Although incentive rewards are not presented until *after* the goal has been achieved, they function most effectively when they are *known to exist* throughout the work period. For example, employees can be expected to work harder for a ten percent bonus if they know it is promised by management from the beginning of the year than if it comes as a complete surprise at the end of a banner year for the company.

The form of reward incentives must be closely coordinated with the needs and desires of the recipient. It accomplishes little, for instance, to reward a task-oriented individual for three years of service without absence. "So what?" the employee may say, even in the act of receiving the reward. "I'd rather be noticed for what I'm doing, not just that I'm here every day."

Abraham Maslow's hierarchy of needs offers a concise way for leaders to evaluate their employees' individual needs and to plan rewards accordingly.

Some individuals with dominant social needs, as reflected in alteration 1 of the Maslow pyramid, may best be rewarded by a gala social event. Other individuals may shun public display and need instead the chance to fulfill a long-cherished career opportunity through promotion, as represented in alteration 2.

FIGURE 11.1
MASLOW'S HIERARCHY OF NEEDS

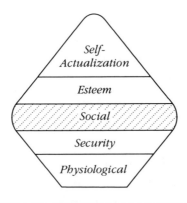

FIGURE 11.2
ALTERATION 1

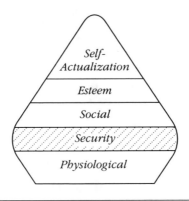

FIGURE 11.3
ALTERATION 2

The point is simply that no single reward in itself is appropriate for all individuals. Leaders must evaluate the "fit" between the intended reward and the needs of the recipient.

In this regard, organizational leaders often perceive rewards and recognition much differently than their subordinates. In a series of studies throughout the 1980s by Paul Hersey and Kenneth H. Blanchard, individuals in leadership roles consistently ranked work experiences very differently than their employees did.[47]

	Supervisors' Ranking	Workers' Ranking
Good working conditions	4	9
Feeling "in" on things	10	2
Tactful disciplining	7	10
Appreciation for work done	8	1
Management loyalty to workers	6	8
Good wages	1	5
Promotion and growth with company	3	7
Understanding of personal problems	9	3
Job security	2	4
Interesting work	5	6

Priority of Wanted Job Aspects (1 = highest)

The fact that supervisors ranked "good wages" first on their list while employees ranked "appreciation for work done" first should serve as a wake-up call to any leader responsible for devising meaningful rewards for workers. The dollars attached to the reward do not necessarily determine its impact.

A final consideration in designing and dispensing rewards has to do with *equity*. Employees in an organization inevitably know through the grapevine approximately what rewards each is receiving and what work is being done for those rewards. When a leader presents a reward of any kind to an employee, that reward is immediately evaluated by the recipient and by his or her peers in relation to its equity or fairness to all concerned.

Let's say, for example, that Salesperson A, after a lackluster three quarters, sells 5,000 units in a great fourth quarter and receives a company reward with the accompanying hoopla. Salesperson B, however, has sold a steady 1,500 units for each quarter of the year and receives no recognition.

According to J. Stacey Adams, the father of the equity theory of motivation, this situation might prove demotivating to most members of the organization.[48] The reward to Salesperson A implies that a big splash is valued more in the organization than steady contribution. Adams's formula for evaluating perceived equity can be explained as follows:

None of us feels cheated if a company superstar receives just rewards for outstanding accomplishments. But all members of any organization, including the reward recipient, can feel uncomfortable and dispirited when rewards are distributed without due consideration of the relative contributions of all group members. Morale suffers and motivation flags when rewards are serendipitous.

Leadership Tips

1. Make frequent use of the least expensive reward for achievement: recognition in a suitable public forum by a respected authority figure.

2. Be sure that rewards available for achievement are known throughout the work period leading to that achievement.

3. Match rewards to the needs and desires of the recipient while maintaining equitable standards in the eyes of the group.

12

The Encouragement Role (2): Support

You have to be very careful that you don't punish people for taking chances. . . . You make it very clear that the people who go out there and are the pioneers who try things shouldn't be punished if it fails.

Tom Stemberg,

CEO, Staples

Sara Lee, a seventeen-billion-dollar company perhaps most known for its frozen
cheesecake, also is the parent company for
Hanes underwear, Kiwi shoe polish, Jimmy
Dean sausages, Ball Park hotdogs, Playtex
undergarments, and Coach leather products,
among many others. Paul Fulton served as
president of Sara Lee from 1988 to 1993. He
comments on the difficult task of managing
decision-making in a company blessed or
cursed, depending on one's perspective, with
such a varied product line.

"We can't worry about local decisions,"
says Fulton, "but what we can do is really
create people who understand how to think
about and make those decisions for us. We
teach Sara Lee managers how to think about
and understand brands and consumers. We
give them a reasonable portfolio of products
and brands to deal with. We visit them. We
listen. We coach. We suggest. We move them
around some, between countries and across
divisions and functions, to expose them to
new ideas and processes.[49]

Paul Fulton's challenge of "controlling" the actions
and attitudes of subordinates across several continents
and more than a dozen product lines happens more
through support than commands. Leaders like Fulton
reward and encourage desired performance by the type
of support they provide to their employees.

Such supportive leadership, as studied most prominently by R. J. House and T. R. Mitchell, is most effective in work situations that are perceived by employees as tedious, stressful, and risky.[50] The leader's efforts to provide meaningful forms of support in such circumstances (as detailed below) can have the result of lowering anxiety, increasing comfort levels, if not interest, with the tasks at hand, and minimizing perceived dangers of the work.

As might be expected, supportive leadership is less meaningful when workers enjoy what they are doing and are confident of success. Support offered by the leader in these cases is perceived as a "nice-to-have," but not a "must-have" for a productive work environment.

Support from the leader can come in tangible forms: state-of-the-art equipment, conducive work environment, sufficient staff, access to necessary information, desirable work schedules, and so forth. But most research on supportive leadership has focused on the less tangible but often more influential form of support proffered by an understanding, considerate, and helpful leader.

A leader who lets subordinates know that he or she cares about their work experiences, understands the obstacles they face, and is committed to working for their welfare can exert a positive influence on the entire organization. Employees feel more job satisfaction (with a resultant drop in absenteeism and turnover) when they feel personally supported in their work efforts by their leader. General stress levels in the workplace are lowered, bringing about less drug abuse and fewer stress-related illnesses and injuries. Most important, production levels rise as supportive relations with management breed mutual dedication to organizational goals and shared willingness to meet company challenges and crises.

The following guidelines provide specific behaviors for leaders who want to be perceived as supportive influences in the work lives of their employees.

1. *Avoid comments and behaviors that can be magnified into unintended messages.* Any words or nonverbal signals sent by the leader to an employee (because of the differing power relations between the two) can be magnified into a message the leader would not recognize. A CEO, for example, might walk into the office and grumble something about "people pulling their own weight" to an employee in the hall. That comment, intended simply to express some general dissatisfaction with recent company performance, can easily be taken personally by the listener, who may brood over the words as if they were the precursor to termination.

Words of praise from the leader can similarly be overinflated and misapplied by listeners if those words are not clear in their reference and precise in their terms. A leader who tells assembled employees that "we've scored the ultimate victory over our competitors" may face a crew for the next several weeks more willing to rest upon their laurels than to press on to higher performance levels.

2. *Demonstrate concern for the whole person in relationships.* Employees are quick to realize when caring on the part of the leader extends only to their utility for purposes of work. A leader who inquires about a stocking clerk's hurt ankle must do so in a way that avoids the subtext, "How soon can you get back on the job?" Especially in an era when more than half (54 percent) of working women care for one or more children under five, leaders must be flexible in their approach to work scheduling and emergency absences if they want to retain some of their best workers.

Executives at Honeywell took this aspect of supportive leadership with great seriousness when, in a company-wide survey of women employees under age 35 who had children, more than *half* agreed with this statement: "I am usually too tired or stressed from work to effectively address my family's day-to-day problems."[51] Leaders hoping to escape the inordinately expensive "hire-train-birth-quit-hire" cycle for women must demonstrate concern for the whole person, not just the person they see from 8 to 5.

3. *Maintain supportive relationships by frequent reinforcement.* Leaders are never so full of sanguine thoughts and good wishes as they are at new employee orientation sessions. Unfortunately, that is often the last occasion when employees hear a good word from the company leader. Supportive relationships aren't established once for life, like an emotional vaccination. Instead, they require care and feeding.

Although few corporate leaders in larger companies can maintain the number of personal relationships with the work force as they might wish, these leaders can remind their vice presidents, directors, managers, supervisors and others to keep up a steady flow of encouraging comments, appreciative remarks, and concerned questions to the workers under their authority. Some of the most progressive and successful companies build this aspect of managerial performance into the job description itself, and they hold company leaders at all levels responsible for nurturing supportive relationships in their work areas.

4. *Offer assistance in a way that will not be perceived as a lack of confidence.* The old advice was for a leader to pitch in whenever the workload mounted to unusual levels for the workers. However well intentioned, these efforts sometimes sent a countermessage: "You guys can't handle things when the heat's on." Workers end up feeling chagrined rather than impressed at their leader's rolled-up-shirtsleeves assistance.

Leaders can avoid this embarrassment for all concerned by bringing in temporary help or taking on low-priority tasks while leaving the high-visibility jobs to the work force. Especially when workers are stressed by a heavy workload, they don't want to be shown "how to do it" by an interloping leader.

5. *Speak well of the employee to others.* Most organizations have a fine-tuned grapevine that communicates bad news and critical judgments much faster than

good news and compliments. When a leader makes a disparaging remark about an employee, even in confidence or "off the record," that news (usually in exaggerated form) inevitably gets back to the employee.

Leaders should be extremely careful, therefore, in making negative comments about their workers, even when those comments are couched in humor or wit. What can be said well about an employee is much more important to share with others. That compliment, when it reaches the employee through the grapevine, will come as an encouraging, motivating influence.

Leadership Tips

1. Recognize that, as a leader, your words and actions stand at the small end of a public megaphone: what you do or don't do will be magnified in importance, for better or worse.

2. Offer support in a way that says "You deserve it!" rather than "You need it!"

3. Consider support as a program, not a gesture. Don't begin to provide necessary support, only to withdraw it in midstream.

13

The Information Role (1): Communication Design and Monitoring

Today's organization is typically a 20/80 place, with only 20 percent of the people involved being employed full-time by the organization. The others are suppliers or contractors, part-timers, or self-employed professionals. More and more, the organization is a "box of contracts" rather than a home for life for all its people.

Charles Handy[52]

In the mid-1980s, Sun Microsystems, Inc., now with 14,000 employees spread over twenty-seven countries, found itself hamstrung internally and externally by paper-bound communication. Under the leadership of CEO Scott McNealy, Sun set itself the task of becoming a "paperless organization" in which virtually all communications and transactions would take place by phone or e-mail.

As the expression goes, be careful what you wish for. You may get it. By 1995, Sun's employees were sending an average of 150 messages per day per employee. One software sales manager reported coming back to 452 e-mail messages after a three-day business trip. What began in the mid-1980s as the paper blizzard has turned into an electronic snowstorm in the 1990s and beyond.

Sun is acting now to install a more sophisticated e-mail system that allows prioritization of messages. It is also developing a "message culture" among its employees that sends succinct messages only to those with a need to know.

Information that can't reach its intended audience efficiently soon becomes misinformation or, worse, disinformation. The responsibility falls to leaders to establish and nurture effective channels of information within their organizations. In other words, leaders are responsible for the *communication design* for their companies. Viewed as architecture, communication in the company takes on dimensional characteristics. The leader determines how best to manage *up, down,* and *sideways* within the organization. In addition, the leader oversees and participates in the *monitoring, informing, consulting,* and *mentoring* functions of the successful organization. (The latter three topics are discussed in Chapter 14.)

As Max DePree has written, these matters lie at the heart of any organization's concern for quality: "We talk about quality of product and service. But what about the quality of our relationships and the quality of our communications and the quality of our promises to each other?"[53]

COMMUNICATION DESIGN

In developing a design or architecture for communication within an organization, the leader can be guided by three watchwords:

1. *"There is no such thing as no communication."* Subordinates who receive no news from the company leader don't assume that the leader has nothing of great importance to communicate. Instead, they usually fabricate powerful messages: that the leader is out of touch with company needs or that they, the employees, don't matter to the leader.

2. *"More communication is not necessarily better communication."* In a business era when managers across industries are experiencing a "word blizzard" from voice-mail, e-mail, faxes, pagers, letters, memos, and reports, more communication may in fact become a disruption to the accurate, timely interpretation of business messages. A leader's goal is to establish meaningful channels of communication that don't overload the message recipient.

3. *"Data are not information."* A flow of factual material of any kind, whether in numbers or prose, does not become information until it truly *informs* the message recipient. Communication design must take into consideration not only the intentions of message senders but also the interpretive capacities and capabilities of the message receivers.

Communicating Up

Communication flows upward in an organization in both structured and unstructured ways. Among the most common forms of structured upward communication are quality circles, focus groups, a variety of reports (progress, periodic, trip, investigation, etc.), suggestion boxes, employee surveys, ombudspersons, and information passed forward to management by labor unions.

Unstructured forms of communication are no less common and certainly no less valuable: conversations with company leaders as they "walk the talk" by their presence throughout the workplace; information purposely or accidentally leaked to leaders from the employee grapevine; and messages communicated by action, such as work slowdowns, turnover, and absenteeism.

Healthy channels of upward communication allow leaders to keep themselves informed of company problems, progress on projects, and opportunities for better use of human and financial resources. The advantages of upward communication to employees include the chance to participate in company decision-making, to attain a broader perspective on company challenges and realities, and to extend their own abilities as problem-solvers and potential leaders.

But an overload of upward communication can devastate the organization in at least three ways. First, valuable leadership time is consumed in reviewing large amounts of upward communications, much of which may be redundant. Company leaders need time for reflection and consultation for effective decision-making. Second, company leaders may be tempted to micromanage even the most trivial matters in corporate life if they are apprised of each and every problem or situation that occurs in the ranks.

Finally, employees can become demoralized if the company leader encourages upward communication, but then does nothing with it (and often fails to review or scan it). For example, many companies send out employee surveys on a regular basis; but employees often complain that, far from seeing any action from the company, they seldom even hear of the results of these surveys.

Leadership expert Warren Bennis recalls his own confrontation with a virtual snowstorm of upward communication when he served as president of the University of Cincinnati.

> My moment of truth came toward the end of my first ten months. It was one of those nights in the office. The clock was moving toward four in the morning, and I was still not through with the incredible mass of paper stacked before me. I was bone weary and soul weary, and I found myself muttering, "Either I can't manage this place or it's unmanageable." I reached for my calendar and ran my eyes down each hour, half-hour, quarter-hour to see where my time had gone that day, the day before, the month before. . . . My discovery was this: I had become a victim of a vast amorphous, unwitting, unconscious conspiracy to prevent me from doing anything whatever to change the university's status quo.

From this experience, Bennis drew his First Law of Academic Pseudodynamics: "Routine work drives out nonroutine work, or: how to smother to death all creative planning, all fundamental change in the university or any institution."[54]

Communicating Down

Most forms of downward communication come naturally to leaders, some of whom seem to believe this is the *only* form of company communication. Downward communication includes verbal directives, memos, policies, procedures, training materials, assignments, performance evaluations, and company magazines and newsletters.

Leaders like the channels of downward communication because they seem to be efficient ways to initiate action in the work force. These channels are also effective ways to distribute company information as widely as possible to employees, with minimal distortion.

However, a misuse or overabundance of downward communication can breed the "waiting-for-instructions" syndrome among employees, who gradually give up independent initiative. Furthermore, employees who are deluged by downward communication may begin to turn a deaf ear and blind eye to messages from the leader. This has been called the "bulletin-board dilemma" in which the bulletin board is plastered with executive messages that go unread by employees, even though these workers pass by the bulletin board every day.

Modern leaders face the growing dilemma of communicating with stakeholders who are not, in the traditional sense, under their complete authority. John Sculley, former CEO of Apple, puts the case well:

> The new model [for leadership] is global in scale, an interdependent network. So the new leaders face new tests such as how to lead people who don't report to them—people in other companies, in Japan or Europe, even

competitors. How do you lead in this idea-
intensive, interdependent-network environment?
It requires a wholly different set of skills, based
on ideas, people skills, and values.[55]

Communicating Sideways

Leaders establish the channels and occasions for structured lateral communication among their employees.
For example, a company leader may determine which
division heads will convene for a meeting and may well
dictate the core agenda of that meeting. The company
leader can also mandate the degree to which divisions
within the company make other divisions aware of
their work through "FYI" copies of reports, briefings,
and liaison employees.

Leaders have less influence, however, on unstructured lateral communications in their organizations.
These contacts occur at lunches, after-hours socializing,
unofficial phone conversations, and all the other communication opportunities available through the company grapevine.

Leaders encourage a certain amount of lateral
communication among company employees at all levels to build an inclusive team spirit throughout the
company, undo latent "us-against-them" rivalries between company divisions, and promote intergroup
information sharing and problem-solving.

Uncontrolled lateral communication can cut deeply
into each employee's worktime (as each employee tries
to keep up with the message flow from all the other

divisions), can undermine the control of the company leader by spreading divisive or subversive information, and can intensify division battles over limited resources, as the details of "who got what" are sent throughout the company. In terms of resource allocation, "a lot of knowledge is a dangerous thing" at times. Many company leaders prefer to hold salary information, division budgets, and other sensitive information close to the vest as a way of avoiding jealousy and in-fighting among company employees and work units.

MONITORING

Leaders monitor information not only about internal aspects of their organizations but also about environmental factors external to the organization. This activity is not passive—leaders don't monitor with an eye to the keyhole or ear to the door. Instead, effective monitoring is an active intellectual inquiry into company procedures, processes, and assumptions.

For example, when Lary Evans was vice president of manufacturing at Tandem Computers, he and his team dramatically reduced the time it took to manufacture one of Tandem's most successful products, the Tandem Non-Stop. His secret as a leader and his recommendation? "Well," he said, "the first thing you've got to do is challenge the process all the time."[56] Leaders refuse to accept obstacles imposed by tradition. By monitoring all factors that contribute to or detract from mission success, they determine the best way to reach their production goals.

Leaders can accomplish internal monitoring in the following ways, among others:

- Conducting meetings to check progress, learn about problems, and gain information
- Performing quality control inspections of products and services
- Visiting work facilities on a regular basis to observe operations and personnel
- Receiving reports and briefings about projects and processes
- Accessing computer information about performance data
- Talking to individual employees about their performance and insights

Environmental monitoring is accomplished in many ways:

- Customer surveys and questionnaires
- Congenial relations and frequent exchanges with government agencies and regulators
- Contacts with competitors and those in allied industries through professional associations
- Magazines, journals, books, and other materials on company-related topics
- Sampling of competitors' products and services

The consequences of insufficient or inaccurate monitoring are serious for the organization. If projects are running late or over budget, if employee morale is low, if market conditions are changing, or if customers are dissatisfied, the leader must often act quickly to prevent significant business losses. A leader who fails to take the pulse of the organization with care may often fail to reward the true performers in the company and unfairly reward those who have not contributed.

Several studies have demonstrated that monitored organizations perform better than unmonitored organizations. In particular, a 1990 study compared twenty-eight British companies whose leaders spent considerable time monitoring market conditions, customer preferences, and other external circumstances with twenty-eight companies whose leaders did not monitor these influences. The monitored group of companies performed significantly better than the unmonitored firms.

Leaders can monitor internal aspects of their organizations in all of the following ways:

1. *Seek out multiple information sources.* Without discounting information from the work units themselves, leaders should seek additional independent sources of information on production levels, personnel qualifications, and other factors tied to effective operations. Leaders often use an "open-door policy" or cafeteria meetings with lower-level subordinates as a way of cultivating these additional sources of information.

In doing so, leaders must recognize that they may not "tune in" immediately to what others are trying to tell them. President Jimmy Carter, reflecting on his years of leadership, concludes that leaders "have a duty to understand the needs of people who depend on them. I've never been a victim of racial discrimination. I've never been deprived of basic human rights. I've never suffered from hunger or lack of shelter. As a businessman, a church leader, and a political leader, I became intensely aware of the needs of others in the deep South during segregation, although I wasn't always as courageous as I should have been in trying to alleviate these problems. But understanding the needs and suffering of others is a vital element for successful leadership."[57]

2. *Discover accurate barometers of work performance.* Leaders sometimes make the mistake of trusting one or two measurement standards, only to discover that those indicators do not reflect crucial changes in profits, operating efficiency, or workplace morale. Company leaders at all levels of responsibility should define several measures that can be monitored often to gauge accurately the progress or problems facing the work unit or company.

3. *Meet often with carefully selected group members.* Part of the American leader's antipathy toward meetings (consider Peter Drucker's comment, "We can meet or we can work. We can't do both at the same time."[58]) is the common failure to invite the appropriate participants to the meeting. Leaders can dramatically increase the information they receive in meetings if

they assiduously select only those participants who have a reason to attend. This probably will mean smaller meetings, where more can be shared because participants feel free to speak up.

The location for meetings can often influence the type and quality of information shared there. Retired Representative Norman Shuman (R-California) recalls conversations in the Congressional Cloak Room, which is like a small lounge. "In that setting," he explains, "you could walk up to somebody and say, 'Hey, Bill, how are you going to vote on such-and-such a bill?' 'Why do you want to vote that way?' 'Don't you know about this, did you hear about that?' It was a very open atmosphere; those kinds of deals were expected to be made in the Cloak Room."[59]

4. *Tune in to the grapevine.* This communication channel, of course, was not intended for use by organizational leaders. Learning to gain information from this network of fact, rumor, opinion, and speculation requires both subtlety and patience on the part of a leader. Two communication experts recommend these three approaches to tuning in to the grapevine:

> Make sure, in your involvement with the grapevine, that you make contact in several different places. If you are a midlevel manager, for example, don't restrict your casual knowledge of what others say to the bits and pieces you hear from other midlevel managers. Find interesting associates at other levels in the company. (Sometimes this involvement may entail a new patience level. As Max DePree writes,

"If you want the best things to happen in corporate life, you have to find ways to be hospitable to the unusual person."[60])

Make time (don't just wait for a convenient time) to tune in to the grapevine. In the same way that you block out time for reading important structured communications such as reports and letters, set aside time for regular contact with key people in the company grapevine. These contacts need not, and probably should not, be scheduled as formal meetings of any sort. Instead, mark your calendar with likely times to find your key people at coffee or relaxing after work.

Participate in the grapevine in a natural way. Don't lecture or spy. The grapevine grows through trust and mutual need. It will not include you if you openly stand on a soapbox or take notes on opinions being expressed. Take your lead from others in the grapevine, and be yourself. Both the information you get and the influence you exert will be richer for your effort.[61]

5. *Visit the worksite often unannounced.* Employees will have a natural tendency to "dress up" in behavior and attitude if they know in advance that a company leader will visit their facility. An unannounced visit by the leader, without an inhibiting retinue of assistants, can give the leader an unretouched image of operations and personnel. At the same time, this kind of visit can encourage casual, unrehearsed conversations with workers at all levels.

Depending on the organization's culture, the leader may want to meet first with the work unit manager before walking the floors. It is often advantageous, however, to meet directly with employees (and thereby dignify their opinions) before meeting with their boss. The late Sam Walton maintained a remarkable record of visiting each of the hundreds of WalMart stores at least once a year for candid conversations with employees at all levels.

Betsy Sanders, now a vice president with Nordstrom's, recalls one memorable occasion early in her career when Bruce Nordstrom showed up unannounced in the store. "I was in my department busily working one day when all five of the executive officers of the company started trooping through the department. And then, to my dismay, I saw Bruce Nordstrom get the most terrible frown on his face, shake his head in disgust, and walk over toward me. He came over and he said, 'Betsy, I just overheard a conversation that really has me upset. See those two ladies over there? They were just saying how disappointed they were. Would you go find out what we did to upset them and make it right?' "

Sanders informed the women of Nordstrom's personal concern. "They were delighted to know that he cared. Well, as it turned out, the two women had fallen in love with the dresses in the Gallery—the expensive dress department—but felt they couldn't afford the prices." Sanders worked with the women to find suitable dresses in a moderate price range. "I was really impressed with Bruce Nordstrom," she says. "But

more so when he returned hours later from a nego-
tiating meeting that had certainly taken all of his time
and attention and came back to check with me to find
out what those customers had wanted and what I did
about it."[62]

6. *Welcome bad news as much as good news.* Many
surveys indicate that employees tend to hide problems,
failures, and other forms of bad news from their supervisors, even when such news could save the company from misdirected efforts and wasted resources.
Leaders should interpret failure for their employees in
the way research scientists view negative results from
an experiment: valuable information is gained and
learning is advanced.

Yoshihisa Tabuchi, president and CEO of Nomura
Securities Co., Ltd., of Japan, points out that occasional
mistakes, failures, and bad news in all its forms can
be a renewing, invigorating force for a company:

> If you look at our history, you'll see that we
> have succeeded in everything we have tried.
> We haven't had a failure. To me that is a
> weakness. I think Nomura needs a failure. Past
> success can be as much a trap as a guide.
> Markets today are very volatile; the world can
> change in a day. But some people at Nomura
> believe that the way we succeeded in the past
> is the way to succeed in the future. It's natural
> to want to believe that. But unless you tear
> yourself away from that kind of thinking, you
> cripple your ability to cope with change and,
> more important, to create change.[63]

Leaders can monitor environmental influences external to the company by following these guidelines:

1. *Understand your customer's business.* Knowing your customer's business means going beyond your customer's expressed needs for products and services. Leaders can get a valuable head start on product development and service delivery by understanding the obstacles and challenges faced by their customers. At Sun Microsystems, for example, account executives for advanced computer network systems are tasked with knowing their customers' businesses so well that they can participate in solving client business problems.

2. *Learn as much as possible about your competitors' business.* It is human nature, apparently, to ignore or disparage a competitor's product or service as one tries to promote one's own line. Resist this temptation. Leaders must recognize that they stand to gain valuable market information by reading about competitors' products, trying them out, visiting competitors' facilities, and talking to industry experts who know the competitors' products and processes. In this regard, it is helpful to remember that half of the companies that made up the *Fortune 500* list in 1980 were not on the list in 1990. Monitoring changing conditions is a matter of survival.

3. *Delegate monitoring responsibilities.* Even the best-intentioned company leader cannot monitor all the sources of information necessary for formulating sound business strategy and responding to business problems.

Leaders must distribute monitoring responsibilities to other executives in the organization and, if possible, to managers and supervisors as well. This network must be established in such a way, however, that sensitive information can be handled confidentially. In addition, information gathered through delegation must reach its destination at the leader's desk regularly and expeditiously.

4. *Define the most relevant aspects of the external environment for monitoring.* Each industry or organization is sensitive to its own set of external influences. For some businesses, demographics such as the Age Wave or the rise in single-parent households is of crucial importance. For others, international currency variations spell the difference between profit and loss. Leaders must evaluate which of the many external environmental factors matter most for company success.

5. *Act upon the information you gather.* Monitoring is not an end unto itself. The results of monitoring must be tied directly to business strategy and day-to-day operations.

Professor James M. Burns, in *Leadership,* makes the telling point that "the ultimate test of practical leadership is the realization of intended, real change that meets people's enduring needs."[64] Through accurate monitoring of external environments, leaders determine those enduring needs and make plans to fulfill them.

Leadership Tips

1. Take time to sketch out the communication design of your organization. Where is communication traffic heaviest? Why? Where is it lightest, or perhaps nonexistent? Where should changes be made?

2. Broaden your present channels by which you monitor internal and environmental sources of information important to the company. Include sources of information you would prefer not to hear.

3. To inform others effectively, separate unimportant messages from important ones and fit all messages to their intended recipients.

14

The Information Role (2): Informing, Consulting, and Mentoring

How do you build a frog? Do you study the
croak, the prodigious leap, the hyperbolic eyes?
No, you study the pond.

Anonymous Human Resource

specialist at AT&T

Thomas Petzinger, in *The Wall Street Journal* (March 15, 1996), reports on informing, consulting, and mentoring in one rising company:

The system worked almost perfectly—until a truck driver dented a customer's filing cabinet or a warehouse clerk put the wrong box of toner in a shipment. Then, suddenly, a customer-service representative was pitted against a loading-dock manager, turning fellow employees into adversaries.

"We've got an angry customer up here!" came the cry from customer service.

"Hey, you have no idea of the headaches I've got down here," came the answer from the loading dock.

Jane Biering inherited this problem when she became a division vice president at Staples Inc., the national office-supply retailer. Ms. Biering did not invent the remedy. . . . But she is responsible for something much bigger: nurturing a culture in which employees identify such problems and come up with the solutions.

It's amazing how much your employees know about your operation. It's equally amazing the sense of belonging they experience at the rare companies in which management acts on their cues. This is especially so at a place like Staples, where

the pay is mostly low and the work can
be numbingly routine. "It gets people to
feel a sense of ownership for where they
work," Ms. Biering says.

Mere symbols—a suggestion box, say, or
special parking privileges for the em-
ployee-of-the-month—accomplish nothing. Getting real ideas from employees
demands buoyantly open-minded leadership and the eradication of intimidation.
So Ms. Biering regularly assembles employees at all job levels, encouraging them
to sound off while she dangles her legs
from the edge of a folding table. Says a
telephone clerk named Elaine Rabbitt:
"There's no nervousness in dealing with
Jane."

Jane Biering typifies the corporate leader who knows
the bottom-line value of keeping employees informed,
consulting them often, and mentoring them for job
efficiency and satisfaction.

INFORMING

Many advantages accrue in organizations where leaders
regularly share information with the rank and file:
increased motivation as employees understand the
importance of their jobs in the big picture; quicker
adjustment by employees to changing company circumstances; increased team spirit based on an enlarged
perspective of the company's mission and market

position; and better performance due to clear information on goals, techniques, deadlines, and other matters crucial to efficient operations.

Leaders should consider the following guidelines in putting their *intentions* to regularly inform group members about important company news into daily practice:

1. *Devise ways to distinguish important messages from less important messages.* It comes as a surprise to some organizational leaders that not every word out of their mouths or word processor earns rapt attention from intended listeners or readers. Some companies have developed simple ways to tell the sheep from the goats in messages through a paper color scheme (red messages are urgent, yellow messages are background information, etc.). This scheme can be carried over into e-mail and voice-mail; most contemporary systems allow users to earmark messages as "urgent."

The key, of course, is to restrict this designation for use by company leaders, and then only sparingly. If every message from the company leader is marked "urgent," the net effect for readers is that of crying "Wolf" too often: none of the messages is looked upon as urgent.

2. *Fit the message to the needs of the message recipient.* Company leaders are often guilty of clogging organizational communication channels with a host of unnecessary or misdirected messages. The ease of

sending an e-mail message to everyone on the system tempts many leaders to follow the "it-won't-hurt-them-to-read-it" criterion of message sending instead of targeting specific messages to specific readers.

Jack Welch, CEO of General Electric, recalls his own initial attempts at streamlining the messaging process in his company:

> At our . . . officers' meeting, which involves the top 100 or so executives at GE, we asked the 14 business leaders to present reports on the competitive dynamics in their businesses. How'd we do it? We had them each prepare one-page answers to five questions: What are your market dynamics globally today, and where are they going over the next several years? What actions have your competitors taken in the last three years to upset those global dynamics? What have you done in the last three years to affect those dynamics? What are the most dangerous things your competitor could do in the next three years to upset those dynamics? What are the most effective things you could do to bring your desired impact on those dynamics? Five simple charts.[65]

3. *Create secure ways for employees to get their own information.* Organizational leaders should not position themselves as the company encyclopedia. Resourceful employees can use company libraries and data bases, encrypted for security, if necessary, to find answers to their questions. Certain "firewalls" may have to be established to prevent unwarranted employee

queries into some company files, including personnel matters, sensitive new product information, and the like.

Robert Haas, chairman and CEO of Levi Strauss, Inc., views this enabling or empowering function as a primary characteristic of leadership:

> If the people on the front line really are the keys to our success, then the manager's job is to help those people and the people that they serve. That goes against the traditional assumption that the manager is in control. In the past, a manager was expected to know everything that was going on and to be deeply involved in subordinates' activities. I can speak from experience. It has been difficult for me to accept the fact that I don't have to be the smartest guy on the block, reading every memo and signing off on every decision. In reality, the more you establish parameters and encourage people to take initiatives within those boundaries, the more you multiply your own effectiveness by the effectiveness of other people.[66]

4. *Let employees know that you know what they and their work units are accomplishing.* To do so, suggests Carl Rogers in *On Becoming a Person,* try "saying back" to others what they have been saying, in one way or another, to you. If assembly-line workers have a good idea for increasing production, the leader's approving reference to that suggestion in a general memo or company newsletter serves to recognize achievement and increase team spirit.

5. *Be prompt in letting all stakeholders know about company decisions, agreements, and changes.* Employees at all levels rightly judge their stature within the organization by the order in which they receive important company information relative to others. A fast, accurate information system emanating from the leader's office can forestall workers' feelings of isolation and alienation precisely at those times when the company most depends upon team efforts.

CONSULTING

Leaders consult internally and externally to provide themselves with reliable information for planning and decision-making. Typical internal consultation occurs in one-on-one or group meetings with the executive team, division heads, and other employees. From these meetings the leader gleans vital information about company problems, prospects, capabilities, and progress.

A more narrow form of consultation occurs in goal-setting sessions with employees. The leader negotiates, in effect, a work contract that will serve to direct the employee's activities for a specific term, as well as provide a standard by which the employee's performance can be judged.

External consulting involves the leader in a wide range of conversations, conferences, and other forms of information-sharing with any person or group with valuable insights to share that might influence the company positively or negatively.

For example, consultation with government representatives may provide the leader with early warning of legislation that will affect company operations or marketing. Consultation with business attorneys can yield crucial information about litigation trends with regard to product liability, hiring and firing, and patent or copyright changes. Consultation with clients or potential clients can give the leader a clearer idea of how well the organization is fulfilling its current market goals and reveal future opportunities.

Effective consulting habits can become part of the company culture. At Chaparral Steel Corporation, CEO Gordon Forward says, "We make the people who are producing the steel responsible for keeping their process on the leading edge of technology worldwide. If they have to travel, they travel. If they have to figure out what the next step is, they go out and find the places where people are doing interesting things. They visit other companies. They work with universities."[67]

Leaders should consider the following guidelines for participating in both internal and external consulting:

1. *Build trust before requesting information.* Much of the most important information to be had inside or outside the company is highly sensitive. An employee who knows of an ongoing theft problem in the company probably puts himself or herself at considerable risk in discussing the matter with the company leader unless confidentiality is promised and respected. An external industry expert with valuable contacts at several of your competitors may be willing to talk with

you so long as "bridges aren't burned" by your ill-timed or unguarded disclosure of that information.

2. Understand consultation as a two-way street. Parties to consultation expect to get, as well as to give, information. Be prepared, therefore, to be candid in your discussion and open to compromise and flexibility.

3. Don't expect too much for free. Particularly in external consulting relations, some form of favor, payment, or other compensation is usually an expected part of an information exchange that is worth your time. Some industry experts, for example, will expect to be hired on an hourly or daily basis for their time, and they should be willing to sign a nondisclosure agreement for information they learn about your products, people, and operations.

Others, including government regulators, community leaders, and professional colleagues, may have to be compensated in more subtle ways—an expensive lunch, invitation to membership in a prestigious group or board to which you belong, a golf game with helpful friends, and so forth.

MENTORING

Helping a subordinate or peer to develop useful job skills and attitudes pays dividends all around. The recipient of mentoring becomes more productive in the organization and more promotable to increased levels of responsibility. He or she feels more loyalty to the organization and its employees and is therefore more likely to perform and less likely to quit.

The mentor, too, receives benefits, including a more skilled colleague to assist with current and future work, a closer bond of fellow-feeling with members of the work team, and an insider's view of ways in which managerial and other skills can be imparted to others most efficiently.

Mentoring, narrowly defined, pertains specifically to coaching and development to advance and promote a person's career. Compared to training functions, mentoring targets the comprehensive, transcendental issues of managerial growth—issues such as harmonious working relations with peers, career crises, burnout, collaborative involvement with teams, and so forth.

Perhaps the most difficult aspect of mentoring is teaching others to lead, not to follow. (Mentoring, as practiced by some leaders, actually teaches "followership" more than leadership.) The president of Versatec, Inc., Renn Zaphiropoulos, displays an important framed watchword to all who enter his executive offices: "Do not follow where the path may lead. Go instead where there is no path and leave a trail."[68] In trying to remain true to this rubric, leaders must allow for considerable experimentation, ambiguity, doubt, and even occasional failure on the part of their charges.

Leaders in training often begin by attempting to control circumstances. What they learn through wise mentoring is to control themselves. In the words of Jim Whittaker, the first American to climb Mt. Everest, "You never conquer the mountain. You only conquer yourself." Once that conquest has been achieved, leadership becomes almost inevitable.

Leaders should consider the following guidelines in their efforts to mentor others in their organizations:

1. *Practice what you preach.* Most complex managerial tasks cannot be adequately described as a series of discrete learning steps. "You had to *be there,*" leaders often find themselves saying in an effort to describe a complex experience. Serving as a role model teaches volumes beyond the actual words of guidance spoken by the mentor. The mentor's ways of handling situations through subtleties of voice, gesture, eye contact, listening techniques, timing, and dozens of other matters are all observed by the learner, sometimes in unconscious ways.

This being said, leaders must not present themselves as *perfect* models. It is helpful to remember that Babe Ruth struck out 1,330 times on his way to hitting 714 home runs, and R. H. Macy's spectacular retailing success in New York City was preceded by his seven business failures.

The founder of Common Cause, John Gardner, points out the importance of the leader as a role model for group members:

> A loyal constituency is won when people, consciously or unconsciously, judge the leader to be capable of solving their problems and meeting their needs, when the leader is seen as symbolizing their norms, and when their image of the leader (whether or not it corresponds to reality) is congruent with their inner environment of myth and legend.[69]

Robert Haas, CEO of Levi Strauss, Inc., insists that his top people view themselves as role models:

> The first responsibility for me and for my team is to examine critically our own behaviors and management styles in relation to the behaviors and values that we profess and to work to become more consistent with the values that we are articulating. It's tough work. We all fall off the wagon. But you can't be one thing and say another. People have unerring detection systems for fakes, and they won't put up with them. They won't put values into practice if you're not.[70]

2. *Become a resource to valuable reading, consultation, and development opportunities.* All mentors should reflect on the variety of experiences that contributed to their present stature and abilities in the organization. Once those experiences have been identified, they should be urged upon the person being mentored. In other words, the mentor should not simply offer himself or herself as the "lesson" to be learned, but offer in addition his or her *history* as a valuable resource for managerial development.

For example, the mentor may have attended several career-shaping seminars or read a few deeply influential books. Because these resources have proven their value for the mentor, they should be offered with confidence to the person being mentored.

3. *Interpret the person's experiences as lessons.* Too many developing managers consider the past not as a

prologue but as a problem—the tale of how not to do things. There is a certain logic to this conclusion, of course. People find themselves being mentored in better ways to approach business situations, and they may justly conclude that previous efforts weren't up to snuff. The mentor can undo the discouraging aspects of this negative approach to an individual's personal history by emphasizing that each experience from the past contributed a positive lesson for future growth. By analogy, a bird's first efforts to fly could be interpreted negatively as a series of abject failures or, more appropriately, as a positive and necessary set of experiments plotted on a learning curve leading to mastery.

4. *Provide environments for experimentation with new learning.* The following statement is attributed to Confucius: "I hear and I forget; I see and I remember; I do and I understand." Mentors have not successfully concluded their work until the learner has had several opportunities to apply the new learning. If possible, this learning environment should include most of the challenges and obstacles of real-world business situations, but it should allow some tolerance for the learner's experimentation and initial errors.

Special projects and assignments, for example, give a developing manager the chance to try out new skills without sinking the company ship if things do not go well. Frequent debriefing sessions with the mentor both during and after the learning experience help the developing manager make sense out of the experience and apply its lessons to more challenging work.

"I talk with people all over the country about learning organizations, and the response is always very positive," says the CEO of Hanover Insurance companies, William O'Brien. "If this type of organization is so widely preferred, why don't people create such organizations? I think the answer is leadership. People have no real comprehension of the type of commitment it requires to build such an organization."[71]

M.I.T.'s Peter Senge agrees: "In a learning organization, leaders' roles differ dramatically from that of the charismatic decision maker. Leaders are designers, teachers, and stewards. These roles require new skills: the ability to build shared vision, to bring to the surface and challenge prevailing mental models, and to foster more systematic patterns of thinking. In short, leaders in learning organizations are responsible for building organizations where people are continually expanding their capabilities to shape their future—that is, leaders are responsible for learning."[72]

The word *learning*, in fact, may sum up better than any other the key to leadership. *Learning* suggests a set of attitudes—of curiosity, earnestness, and humility—and a set of relationships, characterized by mutual involvement and respect. To lead, as every leader will attest, is to learn.

Leadership Tips

1. Adjust the volume, depth, and frequency of information to the work needs of the recipient.

2. Consider consulting as an opportunity not only to share your expertise but to learn from others.

3. Mentor in such a way that others learn how to lead, not just how to follow.

Instruments for Leadership Development

Working through these 20 questions and diagnostic exercises will help you relate the content of this book to your own leadership development. You will spot areas for personal work in becoming the best leader you can be.

1. On one 3" × 5" card, write down your vision for your organization.

2. If several of your organization's members were asked to describe your vision for the organization, what would they say? Why?

3. List three oral means (such as meetings or speeches) by which you share with others your vision for your organization.

4. List three written means (such as memos or newsletter articles) by which you let others know your vision for the organization.

5. Whom do you consider members of your immediate team at work? How well does that team function? What is your role in the team?

6. How are teams formed and managed in your organization? What is your personal role in that process? Should your role change? How?

7. Who designed the personnel structures and organization chart in your organization? When? Do these designs support or inhibit your leadership efforts? What changes are necessary?

8. How have your personal and professional networks changed in the two years? What efforts are you making to build networks helpful to your organization?

9. Describe the decision-making process for significant matters in your organization. Do you want to be more influential in that process? In what ways?

10. Recall the last three important tasks that you delegated. How did they turn out? If less than successfully, what could you have done in the delegation process to improve these results?

11. How do you typically find out about conflict within your organization? How do you tend to respond? What other responses might be helpful to the individuals involved and to the organization?

12. How are formal work descriptions used in your organization? Do they reflect actual job responsibilities? If they need updating, how can you extend your leadership influence through that revision process?

13. How do you typically demonstrate recognition for achievement in your organization? What else could you do?

14. What incentives do you and your organization use to motivate performance? What other incentives should you consider?

15. In what specific ways do you support the work activities of others?

16. Who in your organization needs your support but does not receive it? Why? What can be done?

17. On a single sheet of paper, sketch out a general flowchart of communication channels in your organization. What conclusions regarding leadership can you draw from this flowchart?

18. By what means do you monitor the flow of information and communication within your organization? How successful is that monitoring? How can it be improved?

19. What consulting relations should you nurture to enhance the quality of your leadership?

20. Name three people you have mentored in some way in the past year. What have been the results of such mentoring? How could the mentoring process be improved?

Leadership Tools

The following instruments can help leaders at all levels obtain valuable feedback from those they supervise. Some instruments are self-assessments to aid the leader in appraising his or her strengths and weaknesses in leadership roles.

1 Appraising Leadership

Directions: Indicate the characteristics of the leader by circling the number on each 5-point scale that best expresses your evaluation.

1. Allows other to make important decisions	1	2	3	4	5	Makes most important decisions alone
2. Shows respect for sub-ordinates	1	2	3	4	5	Has low opinion of most subordinates
3. Promotes and rewards creativity	1	2	3	4	5	Insists upon traditional approaches
4. Gets input from group members for most decisions	1	2	3	4	5	Seldom solicits input from group members
5. Asks for feedback	1	2	3	4	5	Avoids feedback
6. Tries to develop others	1	2	3	4	5	Concentrates on work tasks, not development of others
7. Praises others for good work	1	2	3	4	5	Seldom praises others
8. Encourages reasonable risk-taking	1	2	3	4	5	Allows little risk-taking
9. Relates as a team player	1	2	3	4	5	Stands aloof from others
10. Values learning from work experiences	1	2	3	4	5	Practices business as usual

Add all circled numbers: _____

This instrument can be best interpreted by reviewing the actual responses of group members. For a more summary interpretation, use the following guidelines:

Score:
- 10–20 You are a team-builder and developer of human assets
- 21–30 You tend toward developmental leadership styles
- 31–40 You tend toward directive leadership styles
- 41–50 You lead in directive ways with little concern for the development of group members

2 Leadership Choices: Empowerment or Direction?

Directions: For each question, circle one letter that best expresses your opinion. When you have answered all questions, transfer your answers to the scoring sheet provided.

Note: This instrument can be used for self-assessment by a leader or can be administered to group members to discover their expectations of a leader.

It's more important for strong leaders in organizations:

1. a. to give workers responsibility and authority
   b. to supervise the work of others carefully

2. a. to teach and learn
   b. to manage and direct

3. a. to make most important decisions alone
   b. to involve group members in important decisions

4. a. to pay attention to the feelings of workers
   b. to focus primarily on the performance of workers

5. a. to show by example what hard work and long hours mean
   b. to delegate tasks efficiently

6. a. to encourage skilled workers to find best practices for work tasks
   b. to give specific directions on how to complete assigned tasks

7. a. to demonstrate expertise in technical matters
   b. to praise and reward demonstrations of expertise by workers

8. a. to provide time for consensus decision-making by group members
   b. to make executive decisions promptly

9. a. to resolve worker conflicts by personal intervention
   b. to encourage workers to resolve their own conflicts

10. a. to keep workers informed
    b. to keep workers motivated

11. a. to listen to the opinion of workers
    b. to share their experience with workers

12. a. to run a tight ship
     b. to manage a company widely known as a great place to work

13. a. to accept work standards developed by the workers themselves
     b. to set high standards for worker performance

14. a. to reward effort and performance
     b. to reward knowledge and ability

15. a. to hire based on past accomplishments
     b. to hire based on future promise

16. a. to develop mission and vision statements with group members
     b. to develop mission and vision statements alone or with a small
        executive committee

17. a. to call attention to mistakes by workers
     b. to turn quality control over to workers themselves

18. a. to accumulate power
     b. to distribute power

19. a. to anticipate change
     b. to control operations

20. a. to protect the interests of workers
     b. to develop the abilities of workers

SCORE SHEET

Empowering Leadership	*Directive Leadership*
1a _____	1b _____
2a _____	2b _____
3b _____	3a _____
4a _____	4b _____
5b _____	5a _____
6a _____	6b _____
7b _____	7a _____
8a _____	8b _____
9b _____	9a _____

Empowering Leadership	Directive Leadership
10b _____	10a _____
11a _____	11b _____
12b _____	12a _____
13a _____	13b _____
14b _____	14a _____
15b _____	15a _____
16a _____	16b _____
17b _____	17a _____
18b _____	18a _____
19a _____	19b _____
20b _____	20a _____
Totals _____	_____

3 WHAT OTHERS SAY ABOUT ME AS A LEADER

This instrument raises to a conscious level some of a leader's deepest aspirations, apprehensions, and sources of pride.

Directions: Clear your mind of current tasks and responsibilities. Take a moment to relax and think peacefully about some of the people in your life, past and present: past employers and co-workers, past school friends, present superiors and subordinates, and present friends at work and outside work.

Continuing in that relaxed, imaginative mood, respond in writing to each of the following questions. Your answers are for your eyes only. Respond as candidly as possible.

1. If my parents knew what I was doing on the job hour by hour, they would say _____.

2. My professors from college generally regarded me as _____. If they knew what I was doing now, they would say _____.

3. After I've quit or retired, my former co-workers will probably remember the following traits of my personality: _____ _____.

4. If the people I supervised in the past had to decide upon one word or phrase to characterize my leadership style, it would be _____.

5. If the people I now supervise had to rate my effectiveness as a leader on a 1 to 10 scale (10 highest), they would probably agree on the number _____.

6. Those who know me best realize that I (circle one) give my best/ give reasonable effort/give little of my real ability to my present job.

7. Those who hired me for my present position probably feel _____ at how I've carried out my work responsibilities.

8. When the people I supervise compare me to other leaders in the organization, they probably feel that I am _____ _____.

9. If past employers could watch me work hour by hour for a few days in my present job, they would probably feel that_____ _____.

10. When I compare one by one the individuals I supervise with myself, I conclude that _____.

SCORING: Review each of your answers and assign to each a point value from the following scale:

5 — a very positive response
4 — a positive response
3 — a neutral response
2 — a negative response
1 — a very negative response

In the scale, "positive" means complimentary or favorable to you; "negative" means derogatory or unfavorable to you.

Interpret your score as follows:

40–50: You think highly of yourself as a leader, take pride in past accomplishments, and look forward to good interpersonal relationships and a bright future at work.

30–39: You are generally favorable about your activities and relationships at work. You harbor some misgivings, however, about how others rate your performance and leadership style.

20–29: You have a moderately negative view of your activities, relationships, and personal performance in the workplace.

10–19: You are profoundly negative about how others view your leadership and how you yourself think of your work relationships and activities.

Development work: Write out (or discuss with a trusted work associate) your reasons for responding as you did to the questions in this instrument. If your score is in the negative range, come up with specific steps you can take to feel better about yourself as a leader and about others you supervise.

4 Evaluating the Readiness of Those You Lead

Leaders can use the following instrument as a checklist to review how well they have prepared subordinates to handle new assignments or projects.

Directions: Answer "yes" or "no" to each of the following questions. For each "no" answer, develop specific plans for improving the preparation level of subordinates.

1. _____ Is there widespread consensus among your workers that this project is "do-able" within the budget and time limits you have specified.

2. _____ Have you made sure of the availability of all outside consultation, supply sources, and other forms of support necessary for the success of the project?

3. _____ Can you devote enough of your own time to give your team the help it needs in carrying out the project?

4. _____ Do your workers share your perspective on the importance of the project?

5. _____ Have you received necessary sign-offs and assurances from top management to be sure of its support of this project and your team's work on it?

6. _____ Have your subordinates already demonstrated the skill levels necessary for successful work on this project?

7. _____ Have you made all team members aware of the obstacles you foresee in working on the project?

8. _____ Do team members know the process by which action is authorized on their plans and conclusions?

9. _____ Have you shared with all team members your own knowledge or best estimate of sanctions, pay cuts, reassignment, or other negative impact that may follow if their work on the project is not successful?

10. _____ Have you made sure that all team members understand the type and amount of involvement they can expect of you during work on the project?

5 LEADER'S ANALYSIS OF MEETING SUCCESS

Use this instrument to evaluate meetings and make plans for necessary improvements.

Directions: For each item, select a number from the following scale:

1 — Yes
2 — Partially
3 — No

In the "Future Plans" section, write down ways to enhance positive meeting behaviors and improve negative behaviors.

a. _____ Did meeting attendees feel they had accomplished the work set out for the meeting? Future planning: _____

b. _____ Did the meeting leader feel the work of the meeting had been accomplished? Future planning:_____

c. _____ Did the meeting leader succeed at involving all meeting members in discussion? Future planning: _____

d. _____ Was discussion fair and orderly, without "power plays" or lecturing? Future planning: _____

e. _____ Did decisions reflect the consensus views of the meeting members? Future planning: _____

f. _____ Were meeting members willing to volunteer for assignments? Future planning: _____

g. _____ Did the meeting stick to its time limits? Future planning: _____

h. _____ Did the meeting agenda contain the right amount of work for the time available? Future planning: _____

i. _____ Were the right members present at the meeting? Future planning: _____

j. _____ Were members responsible for input on agenda items well-prepared and clear in their presentations? Future planning: _____

k. _____ Were all assignments given to meeting members specific and manageable with the time limits provided? Future planning: _____

l. _____ Did this meeting help to develop the interpersonal and problem-solving abilities of meeting members? Future planning: _____

_____ Total Meeting Score [Over time, leaders should notice meetings moving closer to a perfect score of "12."]

6 The Leader's Relationship to the Team

This instrument has been adapted to apply to team leaders from "The Team-Player Survey," contained in Glenn M. Parker, *Team Players and Teamwork* (Jossey-Bass, 1996).

Directions: Select the one response for each item that most closely expresses your opinion. When you have responded to all items, transfer your answers to the score sheet, then interpret your relation to the team as a Contributor, Collaborator, Communicator, or Challenger. Definitions of each of these styles is provided on the score sheet.

1. When I lead team meetings, I usually
    a. _____ serve as a technical expert for the team
    b. _____ remind the team often of our mission
    c. _____ try to involve everyone in decision-making
    d. _____ point out where I think the team is going astray

2. I consider my most important responsibility as a team leader is to
    a. _____ keep the team on track with our mission
    b. _____ maintain good interpersonal relations among team members
    c. _____ provide necessary objections and "devil's advocate" debate
    d. _____ share my expertise

3. When meetings become stressful for team members, I sometimes
    a. _____ try too hard to be light-hearted and witty
    b. _____ am too blunt in telling team members what I think
    c. _____ give up trying to involve everyone in the meeting
    d. _____ seek the advice of outsiders in understanding team problems

4. When team members experience conflict with one another or with me, I usually
    a. _____ try to get all points of view out in the open
    b. _____ explain my own point of view as clearly as possible
    c. _____ view such conflict as a sign that changes are needed in team processes
    d. _____ try to diffuse conflict by humor or friendliness

5. I believe I am viewed by team members as
    a. _____ a leader sure of the facts
    b. _____ a flexible leader
    c. _____ a supportive leader
    d. _____ an honest and straightforward leader

6. In looking back over my performance as a team leader, I believe that I am often too
    a. _____ driven by expected results
    b. _____ flexible and understanding
    c. _____ sure of my own position
    d. _____ tempted toward quick fixes

7. When the team does not meet expectations, I usually
   a. _____ work harder for participation from all members
   b. _____ call a summit meeting of the team to get back on track
   c. _____ increase my efforts to provide more and better information for the team
   d. _____ insist that the team turn its attention to our goals and mission

8. I have difficulty
   a. _____ criticizing an action that the team unanimously supports
   b. _____ motivating the team to higher standards
   c. _____ expressing ideas and suggestions outside my area of expertise
   d. _____ giving a team member my evaluation of how he or she relates to other team members

9. I think team members look upon me as
   a. _____ a leader with very high standards
   b. _____ a leader who sometimes can see the big picture
   c. _____ a leader more interested in how the team works than in what it accomplishes
   d. _____ a leader obsessed with details

10. In my opinion, problem-solving by team members requires
    a. _____ the participation of all team members
    b. _____ excellent listening skills by team members
    c. _____ courage in asking unpopular and difficult questions
    d. _____ reliable information

11. In assembling a new team, I usually make an effort to
    a. _____ establish casual, friendly relations with team members
    b. _____ focus as soon as possible on goals and procedures
    c. _____ understand the team's expectations of me as their leader
    d. _____ make sure everyone shares the same essential information about the team's assignment or project

12. I sometimes make team members feel that they
    a. _____ aren't being completely honest with me
    b. _____ aren't measuring up to my expectations
    c. _____ don't see the forest for the trees
    d. _____ don't care enough about the feelings of other team members

13. One of my most important roles as team leader is to
   a. _____ achieve results as efficiently as possible
   b. _____ work with the team so that they participate in goal-setting
   c. _____ involve all team members in decision-making
   d. _____ encourage the expression of contrary opinions and ideas

14. In most cases team decision-making should be based on
   a. _____ the original charter or mission statement for the team
   b. _____ whatever the consensus of team members determines
   c. _____ discussion that involves all team members
   d. _____ the merits of the evidence

15. I believe I am sometimes guilty of
   a. _____ worrying too much about how team members interrelate
   b. _____ challenging the team's ideas too severely
   c. _____ forgetting team processes in my eagerness to obtain results
   d. _____ concentrating too much on big picture issues and ignoring smaller team achievements

16. The word or phrase team members would probably use to describe me is
   a. _____ independent
   b. _____ reliable
   c. _____ visionary
   d. _____ sociable

17. In my activities as team leader, I am usually
   a. _____ dependable and hardworking
   b. _____ dedicated and flexible
   c. _____ supportive and friendly
   d. _____ informed and honest

18. What irritates me most about some team members is their failure to
   a. _____ base discussion and decisions on agreed-upon goals
   b. _____ understand the importance of working well together
   c. _____ compromise when necessary to achieve consensus
   d. _____ meet deadlines and live within resource limitations

Transfer your answers to the appropriate spaces below. Note that the order of letters changes from item to item.

Question #	Contributing Leader	Collaborating Leader	Communicating Leader	Challenging Leader
1.	a. _____	b. _____	c. _____	d. _____
2.	d. _____	a. _____	b. _____	c. _____
3.	c. _____	d. _____	a. _____	b. _____
4.	b. _____	c. _____	d. _____	a. _____
5.	a. _____	b. _____	c. _____	d. _____
6.	d. _____	a. _____	b. _____	c. _____
7.	c. _____	d. _____	a. _____	b. _____
8.	b. _____	c. _____	d. _____	a. _____
9.	a. _____	b. _____	c. _____	d. _____
10.	d. _____	a. _____	b. _____	c. _____
11.	c. _____	d. _____	a. _____	b. _____
12.	b. _____	c. _____	d. _____	a. _____
13.	a. _____	b. _____	c. _____	d. _____
14.	d. _____	a. _____	b. _____	c. _____
15.	c. _____	d. _____	a. _____	b. _____
16.	b. _____	c. _____	d. _____	a. _____
17.	a. _____	b. _____	c. _____	d. _____
18.	d. _____	a. _____	b. _____	c. _____
Totals	_____	_____	_____	_____

As a leader, your primary relationship to the team is indicated by the highest total above. In descending order, the other numbers indicate the relative strength of your other relationships to the team. Interpret your scores according to the following category descriptions:

The Contributing Leader is concerned with providing reliable information to the team. This leader sets high standards for personal and team performance. Team members credit this kind of leader with excellent organizational abilities, including management of budgets and schedules. Members may criticize this kind of leader for narrowness of vision and inflexibility.

The Collaborating Leader is concerned with fulfilling the overall goals and mission of the team. This leader works well with others in a "whatever-it-takes" spirit of flexibility. Team members credit this kind of leader with vision and far-ranging intellect. Members may criticize this kind of leader for losing track of details and undervaluing small, but necessary tasks.

The Communicating Leader is concerned with the processes by which the team attains its goals. This leader listens well and encourages participation by all team members. Team members credit this kind of leader with good "people skills" and conflict resolution abilities. Members may criticize this kind of leader for caring more for people and processes than for results.

The Challenging Leader is concerned with enhancing team performance through "gadfly" questions and comments. This leader often disagrees (or appears to disagree) with the approaches, processes, and conclusions of the group. Team members credit this kind of leader with permitting risk and independent judgment. Members may criticize this kind of leader for standing aloof from the group and failing to respect the motives and insights of others.

Notes

1. James MacGregor Burns, *Leadership* (New York: HarperCollins, 1978), p. 2.
2. Warren Bennis and Burt Nanus, *Leaders: The Strategies for Taking Charge* (New York: Harper & Row, 1985), p. 116.
3. Quoted in S. A. Kirkpatrick and E. A. Locke, "Leadership: Do Traits Matter?" *Academy of Management Executive* 5, 2 (1991): 48.
4. Quoted in Frances Hesselbein, Marshall Goldsmith, Richard Beckhard, eds., *The Leader of the Future* (San Francisco: Jossey-Bass, 1996), p. 74.
5. Cited in A. Bell and D. Smith, *Winning with Difficult People* (Hauppauge, NY: Barron's, 1991), p. 64.
6. John Kotter, *The Leadership Factor* (New York: Random House, 1988), p. 15.
7. For a summary of other leadership taxonomies, see Gary Yukl, *Leadership in Organizations,* 3rd ed. (Englewood Cliffs, NJ: Prentice Hall), p. 68.
8. Quoted in Hesselbein, et al., p. 8.
9. Quoted in James Kouzes and Barry Posner, *The Leadership Challenge* (San Francisco: Jossey-Bass, 1987), p. 81.

10. Lee Eisenberg, "Taking the Long, Sharp View," *Esquire,* 1983, 100 (6): 305.
11. J. A. Conger, *The Charismatic Leader* (San Francisco: Jossey-Bass, 1989), p. 218.
12. Kouzes and Posner, p. 79.
13. Ibid., p. 106.
14. John Gardner, *The Moral Aspect of Leadership: Leadership Papers/*5. (Washington, D.C.: Independent Sector, 1987) pp. 10–18.
15. J. L. Pierce and J. W. Newstrom, *Leaders and the Leadership Process* (Boston: Irwin, 1995), p. 231.
16. P. Slater and W.G. Bennis, "Democracy Is Inevitable," *Harvard Business Review* (Sept.–Oct. 1990): 171.
17. Noel Tichy and Ram Charan, "Speed, Simplicity, Self-Confidence: An Interview with Jack Welch," *Harvard Business Review* (Sept.–Oct. 1989): 54.
18. Quoted in Charles M. Farkas and Philippe De Backer, *Maximum Leadership* (New York: Henry Holt, 1996), p. 37.
19. Farkas, pp. 167–68.
20. Alan Webber, "Consensus, Continuity, and Common Sense: An Interview with Compaq's Rod Canion," *Harvard Business Review* (July–Aug. 1990): 129.
21. Robert H. Hayes, "Strategic Planning: Forward in Reverse," *Harvard Business Review* (Nov.–Dec. 1995): 114.
22. For a thorough treatment of equity theories of motivation, see Paul J. Champagne, *Motivation Strategies for Performance and Productivity* (New York: Quorum Books, 1989).
23. Abraham H. Maslow, *Motivation and Personality,* 2nd ed. (New York: Harper & Row, 1970).
24. Cited in D. Smith, *Motivating People* (Hauppauge, NY: Barron's, 1991), p. 18.
25. J. A. Conger, "The Dark Side of Leadership," *Organizational Dynamics* (Autumn 1990): 44.
26. M. L. Marks, "The CEO's Mea Culpa," *Across the Board* (June 1995): 37.
27. Marks, p. 39.

28. For a summary of the advantages of teams in organizations, see R. A. Eisenstat and S. G. Cohen, "Summary: Top Management Groups," in J. R. Hackman (ed.), *Groups that Work (and Those that Don't)* (San Francisco: Jossey-Bass, 1990) pp. 78–88.

29. Kouzes and Posner, p. 29.

30. Ibid., p. 127.

31. "MCI Founder Bill McGowan." *INC.* (August 1986): 29–30.

32. Interview with Norman Shumway, Congressional Representative (retired), California. Conducted by Bruce Brunger, Nov. 16, 1995.

33. Hesselbein, p. 121.

34. David McClelland, *Power: The Inner Experience* (New York: Irvington, 1975), p. 263.

35. Tichy and Charan, p. 56.

36. Cited in G. Yukl, *Leadership in Organizations,* 3rd ed. Englewood Cliffs, NJ: Prentice Hall, 1994), p. 216.

37. I. L. Janis, *Victims of GroupThink* (Boston: Houghton Mifflin, 1972).

38. Ibid., p. 32.

39. C. William Pollard, "The Leader Who Serves," in Hesselbein, p. 241.

40. Cited in John Madden, *Hey, Wait a Minute: I Wrote a Book* (New York: Ballantine, 1985), pp. 225–26.

41. Cited in A. Bell and D. Smith, *Winning with Difficult People* (Hauppauge, NY: Barron's, 1991), p. 61.

42. Ibid., p. 61.

43. David Burns, M.D., *The Feel Good Handbook,* cited in A. Bell and D. Smith, *Winning . . . ,* p. 37.

44. Ibid., p. 39.

45. Pollard, p. 246.

46. Vance Packard, *The Pyramid Climbers* (New York: McGraw-Hill, 1962), p. 170.

47. Cited in Bell and Smith, p. 42

48. Cited in D. Smith, *Motivating People,* pp. 5–9.

49. Quoted in Farkas, p. 70.

50. R. J. House and T. R. Mitchell, "Path-goal Theory of Leadership," *Contemporary Business,* 3 (Fall 1974): 84.

51. The Honeywell Work/Life Study, p. 28.

52. Charles Handy, "The New Language of Organizing and Its Implications for Leaders," in Hesselbein, p. 6.

53. Max DePree, *Leadership Is an Art* (New York: Dell, 1989), p. 34.

54. Warren Bennis, "View from the Top," in W. Bennis, *Leadership* (Cincinnati, OH: University of Cincinnati, n.d.), p. 26.

55. Quoted in Warren Bennis, ed., *Leaders on Leadership* (Boston: Harvard University Press, 1992), p. xi.

56. Kouzes and Posner, p. 39.

57. Alan Webber, "Jimmy Carter: The Statesman as CEO," *Harvard Business Review* (March/April 1988): 133.

58. Quoted in A. Bell, *Mastering the Meeting Maze* (Reading, MA: Addison Wesley, 1990), p. 32.

59. Shumway interview.

60. DePree, p. 69.

61. N. Sigband and A. Bell, *Communication for Managers* (Cincinnati, OH: South-Western, 1994), p. 284.

62. Recounted by B. Sanders, "There's No Secret to Serving the Customer." Presentation to the Executive Seminar in Corporate Excellence, Santa Clara University, Oct. 28, 1986.

63. Michael Schrage, "A Japanese Giant Rethinks Globalization: An Interview with Yoshihisa Tabuchi," *Harvard Business Review* (July/Aug. 1989): 122.

64. J. M. Burns, *Leadership* (New York: Harper & Row, 1978), p. 21.

65. Cited in Tichy and Charan, p. 56.

66. Robert Howard, "Values Make the Company: An Interview with Robert Haas," *Harvard Business Review* (Sept./Oct. 1990): 38.

67. Kouzes and Posner, p. 59.

68. Quoted in Alan M. Kantrow, "Wide-Open Management," *Harvard Business Review* (May/June 1986): 99.

69. John Gardner, *The Heart of the Matter: Leader-Constituent Interaction*. Leadership Papers 3 (Washington, D.C.: The Independent Sector, 1968), p. 11.

70. Howard, p. 40.

71. Kouzes and Posner, p. 63.

72. Peter Senge, *The Fifth Discipline* (New York: Doubleday, 1990), p. 134.

Suggested
Readings

Bennis, Warren. *On Becoming a Leader*. Reading, MA:
Addison-Wesley, 1989.

Cleveland, Harlan. *The Knowing Executive*. New York:
E.P. Dutton, 1985.

Cohen, W. A. *The Art of the Leader*. New York: Prentice-
Hall, 1990.

DePree, Max. *Leadership Jazz*. New York: Doubleday,
1992.

————. *Leadership Is an Art*. East Lansing, MI: Michigan
State University, 1988.

Farkas, C. M., and P. De Backer. *Maximum Leadership*.
New York: Henry Holt, 1996.

Fisher, W. P., and C. Bernstein. *Lessons in Leadership*.
New York: Van Nostrand Reinhold, 1991.

Gardner, H. *Leading Minds: An Anatomy of Leadership*.
New York: HarperCollins, 1995.

Gardner, J. P. *On Leadership*. New York: The Free Press,
1990.

Hackman, J. R. *Groups that Work (and Those that Don't)*.
San Francisco: Jossey-Bass, 1990.

Hesselbein, F.; M. Goldsmith; R. Beckhard; eds. *The
Leader of the Future*. San Francisco: Jossey-Bass, 1996.

Kotter, J. P. *The Leadership Factor*. New York: The Free
Press, 1988.

Miller, D. *The Icarus Paradox*. New York: HarperCollins, 1990.

Pierce, J. L., and J. W. Newstrom. *Leaders and the Leadership Process*. Boston: Irwin, 1995.

Schein, E. H. *Organizational Culture and Leadership*, 2nd ed. San Francisco: Jossey-Bass, 1992.

Waterman, Robert H. *Adhocracy: The Power to Change*. New York: W.W. Norton, 1992.

Wheatley, M. J. *Leadership and the New Science*. San Francisco: Berrett-Koehler, 1994.

Wren, J. T., ed. *The Leader's Companion: Insights on Leadership Through the Ages*. New York: The Free Press, 1995.

Yukl, G. *Leadership in Organizations,* 3rd ed. Englewood Cliffs, NJ: Prentice Hall, 1994.

Index

About the Author

Dayle M. Smith holds her Ph.D. in Organizational Communication from the University of Southern California (1984). Smith is Professor of Management at the McLaren School of Business, University of San Francisco, where she teaches MBA and Executive MBA classes in leadership and organizational behavior. Her many articles in recent years have appeared in the *Academy of Management Executive, Human Resource Management, Journal of Staffing and Recruitment, Journal of Speech Communication,* and others.

She is the author of *Motivating People* (Barron's, 1992), *Kincare and the American Corporation* (Irwin, 1992), and *Work/Life Management,* a book forthcoming from Harvard Business School Press. She is co-author of *Winning with Difficult People* (Barron's, 1992). Smith is a well-known leadership speaker and consultant; among her clients are the U.S. State Department, American Stores, Kaiser Permanente, Cost Plus Corporation, China Resources, Ltd., CIA, Santa Fe, Williamsburg Foundation, and the Private Industry Council.